FALMOUTH
IN OLD PHOTOGRAPHS

FROM THE ARCHIVES OF
THE ROYAL CORNWALL
POLYTECHNIC SOCIETY

FRIENDS' SCHOOL, FALMOUTH.

THE QUAKERS, or 'Friends', exerted considerable influence on the development of the town, mainly through the Fox family. Having arrived from Par in the 1760s to take advantage of the opportunities offered by the expanding town and port, George Croker Fox (1727 – 1782) established a dynasty which made an enormous contribution to the business, cultural, charitable and educational life of the district. Foundry industries at Perranarworthal and port activities at Portreath augmented the shipping, commercial, fishing and consular business in Falmouth and many of the large – originally country – houses in the area were built or occupied, and their gardens laid out, by members of the family. Penjerrick, Glendurgan, Trebah, Roscrow, Rosehill, Grovehill, Wodehouse Place, Bank House, Penmere, Goonvrea, Tredrea and, for a short time, Trefusis, have all been Fox houses at some time. In the nineteenth century, decades before education became compulsory, members of the Fox family and other Quakers were instrumental in founding and encouraging charity schools for both adults and children of the town and even after the introduction of compulsory education for children, the Friends' Meeting House at the top of Quay Hill continued as a centre for adult education well into the twentieth century. The buildings shown in this picture are probably in what is now Kimberley Place and still in residential use.

FALMOUTH
IN OLD PHOTOGRAPHS

FROM THE ARCHIVES OF
THE ROYAL CORNWALL
POLYTECHNIC SOCIETY

COLLECTED BY

PETER GILSON

ALAN SUTTON

Alan Sutton Publishing Limited
Phoenix Mill · Far Thrupp · Stroud · Gloucestershire

First Published 1990

British Library Cataloguing in Publication Data

Falmouth in old photographs.
1. Cornwall. Falmouth, history
I. Gilson, Peter
942.378

ISBN 0-86299-719-4

Typeset in 9/10 Korinna
Typesetting and origination by
Alan Sutton Publishing Limited.
Printed in Great Britain by
Dotesios Printers Limited.

CONTENTS

INTRODUCTION

Falmouth is not an old town by Cornish standards. Despite the magnificence of its sheltered natural harbour, there was no urban growth near its mouth before the mid-seventeenth century because of the danger of attack from the sea and the earliest towns on the estuary grew up well inland at Truro, Penryn and Tregony. The only habitations on the site of present-day Falmouth were Arwenack Manor, acquired by marriage in 1385 by the Killigrew family, and Smithick, a small hamlet around a creek one kilometre north of Arwenack.

Pendennis Castle was built on Killigrew land between 1539 and 1543 and, together with St Mawes Castle across the harbour, was part of Henry VIII's south coast defences against the possibility of foreign invasion. Except in times of national emergency, the castle seems to have been badly neglected by the Crown for the first 250 years of its life and there were instances of walls falling down, guns being removed, and the garrison starving and unpaid for long periods. Yet it was considerably enlarged and strengthened in the reign of Queen Elizabeth when Spanish invasion threatened and a large part of the headland was fortified by building an enceinte, or enclosure of nearly four acres, surrounded by a sloping stone wall and a dry moat.

The castle saw serious action only during the Civil War when it was besieged by Cromwell's army for 153 days, and on 17 August 1646 became the last English fortress to surrender. As with Singapore in the Second World War, the Pendennis guns had been sited to withstand attack from the sea so new fortifications – trenches reinforced with timber – had to be built on the landward side of the castle to face Cromwell's army. These 'Hornworks' have left their name on this part of the town to this day.

Further periods of neglect followed the Roundhead occupation and for much of the eighteenth century it seems to have been garrisoned by 'invalids', soldiers too old or too unfit to stand the strain of active service, who, with their families, had to eke out an existence as best they could. When a severe thunderstorm struck the castle in 1717 and its eleven-foot thick walls were breached the damage went unrepaired for over thirty years.

In 1795 the castle was purchased by the Crown from Lord Wodehouse and two years later there arrived a man whose devotion and piety were to change the lives of the castle garrison and many people in the town. Captain Philip Melvill had been captured, imprisoned and tortured during the Indian campaigns of 1779. Retired on his release from captivity because of his serious injuries, he later re-enlisted and was appointed deputy Governor of Pendennis Castle in 1797. He set about improving the lives of his 'invalids' by encouraging them to build houses and cultivate gardens on the flat area of clifftop to the west of the castle. During the Napoleonic threat, he formed the Pendennis Volunteer Artillery from among the townsfolk and later was responsible for starting charity schools for boys and girls in the town. In 1807 he established the Misericordia Society 'for the relief of poor strangers, not otherwise able to obtain it and distressed townsfolk, reduced from comfortable circumstances'. When he died in 1811, aged forty-nine, his funeral was attended by large numbers of townsfolk of all classes and the whole Pendennis garrison. A plaque to his memory may be seen in the parish church today.

For much of the nineteenth century the castle was used as a training ground for detachments of Artillery Militia and, after 1908, by the Territorial Army. During both World Wars it became a Coastal Artillery site but in 1920 the keep was declared an Ancient Monument, taken over by the Commissioners of Works, and opened to the public. Following the Second World War it was reopened in 1946, coincidentally 300 years after the Civil War siege ended.

By the time of the Restoration in 1660 Falmouth had become a port of some significance, with an expanding trade in ships' stores, tin for export and coal, iron, timber and charcoal imports. Shipbuilding and fishing were growing in importance, the latter for export to Mediterranean countries. Prosperity was greatly increased in 1688 when the Post Office selected Falmouth as the home base for its Packet Service, to carry overseas mail to Spain and Portugal when land routes were blocked by continental wars. A port in the south-west was necessary to obviate a long sail down-Channel against the westerly winds and the overwhelming advantages of Falmouth harbour over its rivals were borne out over the next 162 years as the Packets were able to come and go by day or night without hindrance in all except the worst of weathers.

For about sixty years a small number of ships maintained an irregular service to Spain and Portugal but as British influence and trade spread into the Mediterranean and across the Atlantic, new Packet routes came into being until, at its peak in the early nineteenth century, the Service had forty vessels sailing regularly on seven 'stations'. As there was a war involving west European powers for much of the Packets' existence before 1815, losses among its ships as a result of enemy action were common. Armaments were, ostensibly, purely defensive and commanders were instructed: 'You must run where you can; you must fight when you can no longer run; and when you can fight no more you must sink the mails before you strike'. The mail was carried on deck in a weighted bag to facilitate this. Some commanders ignored this instruction and turned pirate when the occasion arose. Other losses resulted from attacks by privateers and from bad weather; one, the *Lady Hobart*, was sunk after a collision with an iceberg in the north Atlantic in 1803.

The presence of the Packet ships in the port encouraged a variety of marine-orientated industries using imported timber, tar, hemp, cordage and canvas and these, together with the supply of food from local farms, were a great stimulus to the local economy. Most occupations in the town were related to shipping in some way, even the hotels and boarding-houses catering largely for Packet passengers who often had to wait several days in the town for their vessel to sail.

Some Packet commanders became folk-heroes, none more so than the local man John Bull, who followed his father, James, into the Service. In the *Marlborough* Packet he successfully fought a French privateer at the harbour entrance, watched by an enthusiastic crowd on Pendennis Point, and on another occasion used his local knowledge when being pursued by a hostile vessel to sail, dangerously, inside the Manacles, leaving his pursuer to run on to these treacherous rocks 10km south of Pendennis Point.

Although officially mail and passenger carriers, many Packet crews carried on an illegal yet lucrative trade in a wide range of goods which varied according to the requirements of their ports of destination. From 1780 onwards, the Post Office tried to put an end to this traffic, as well as to several other abuses, but so corrupt was much of the Packet administration that this proved impossible until 1810 when newly-installed customs officers confiscated the trade goods on two ships preparing to depart and their crews refused to sail. The resulting 'mutiny' resulted in the Packets being moved to Plymouth but so unsuitable was the Devon naval base that the ships returned to Falmouth after only two months. Yet all was not as before. Since its inception in 1688, vessels in the Packet Service had been privately owned and hired from their owners by the Post Office; after the mutiny, the Service gradually passed under naval control. But the naval brigs used were not designed for rough-weather Atlantic sailing and became known in Falmouth as 'coffin ships' when seven were lost in the first few months.

By 1830 the steam engine had begun to write the epitaph of the Falmouth Packet Service, being used on land to deliver mail to other ports by rail, and installed in ships to cancel out all Falmouth's advantages over its up-Channel rivals. Private steamship companies, based on Southampton and Liverpool, took over the carriage of mail on Post Office contract until only the South American mail was carried by sailing ships. Early steamships had to carry enough coal for both outward and homeward passages and the distance to Brazil and back was too long for this until 1850 when steam ships finally replaced the sailing Packets on this route. Thus ended a glorious and profitable period in Falmouth's history which had seen the town extend along the whole waterfront from the Bar to north of Greenbank.

Optimists believed that the Packets would return to Falmouth once the railway arrived but the difficulties and high cost of railway construction through the hilly Cornish landscape delayed its arrival in Falmouth until 1863. The realists had already begun to plan for the post-Packet era with two developments which were to set the pattern for the port's present-day economy: the creation of Falmouth docks and the small beginnings of the town's tourist industry. But this will be shown by the photographs in the following pages and need not be described here.

Early Days

ALL ENGRAVINGS SUCH AS THIS are exaggerated in some respects, no doubt to make them appear more spectacular and more saleable. Here the gradients of Pendennis Point have been made steeper and the castle buildings drawn out of proportion to their surroundings. Nevertheless, such inaccuracies cannot diminish the value of such representations which, apart from paintings and sketches, are the only pictorial evidence available to us up to the mid-nineteenth century. This view of Pendennis Castle, dating probably from the mid-eighteenth century shows clearly the main defensive features of the headland. The castle keep dominates the scene and tends to dwarf the Elizabethan enceinte with its steep stone walls and dry moat. Most interesting, though, because they can no longer be seen, is the depiction, to the right of the castle enclosure, of the Hornworks, defences built to withstand the Civil War siege of 1646, which were only obliterated in the mid-nineteenth century because, to quote a local newspaper, 'they were of greater danger to the defenders than to any prospective enemy'.

This brass of John Killigrew (d. 1567) and his wife Elizabeth may be seen on the floor of Budock Church below the step leading to the altar. In the days before Falmouth came into being, Budock parish stretched eastwards to the shore of Falmouth harbour and the Killigrews worshipped at Budock. The Killigrew succession is complicated by the family habit of naming the eldest son after his father which, in those years most closely linked with the Falmouth story, results in four Johns and two Peters. John (I) inherited one of Cornwall's largest estates, worth £6,000 a year, and before his death in 1567 had rebuilt Arwenack House as 'the finest and most costly in the County'. He was the first Governor of Pendennis Castle. John (II) continued to run the estate, despite his wife's involvement with piracy, while his brothers, Henry and William, went to London and became rich and influential in the Court of Queen Elizabeth. John (III) was a heavy drinker and gambler, suspected of complicity with the Spaniards in their abortive attempt to invade England in 1597, who left the estate impoverished on his death; he was the father in Winston Graham's wonderfully descriptive book, *The Grove of Eagles*. John (IV) spent much of his time and money trying to improve the hamlet of Smithick, a suggestion made to his father by Sir Walter Raleigh in 1596, but this was vigorously opposed by Penryn, Truro and Helston. He was also involved in a costly divorce from his wife, Jane, and when he died without heir in 1633 the estate passed to his brother, Peter (I). Something of a charismatic character, he seems to have survived the Civil War by making himself useful to both sides. Despite the Roundhead occupation, he managed to obtain a grant for a market in 1652, two fairs on 7 August and 11 October each year, and the establishment of a Custom House on land north of Smithick, and became known as 'Peter the Post' by carrying messages to Prince Charles in France before the monarchy was restored in 1660. He was knighted for these services, saw the Borough Charter granted by Charles II and the parish church established, dedicated to King Charles the Martyr. His son, Peter (II) succeeded in 1667 and was opposed by the Corporation of the new Borough in all his efforts to increase the town's prosperity. He helped to build quays near Arwenack in 1670 but was thwarted by the Corporation in his attempt to bring a water supply to these quays. His only surviving daughter, Anne, married Martin Lister, a former officer at Pendennis Castle who assumed the family name in a vain attempt to perpetuate the Killigrew line. After his death in 1745, the title passed through the female line, after two generations, to the Wodehouse family of Kimberley Hall in Norfolk.

ARWENACK MANOR was the home of the Killigrew family from 1385 to soon after 1700. John (I) rebuilt it in 1567 with its lawns running down to the harbour-side but his fine house was burnt down in 1646, just before the siege began. It is uncertain whether this act of destruction was perpetrated by the Pendennis garrison to deny its use to the enemy or by the arriving Roundheads but common sense would suggest the former. The house seems never to have been properly rebuilt after the Restoration but to have been reconstructed very haphazardly into a hotch-potch of unsightly buildings and used at various times as the manor office, barracks for the Submarine Miners, Royal Engineers, headquarters of the Packet Service after the Navy took over and as private residences for many different occupants. In the 1960s it stood empty and was regularly vandalized until very tastefully restored over a number of years to its present attractive condition. It is very unfortunate that more recent development has obscured its view of the harbour, one of the reasons for the Killigrews' choice of the site originally.

THIS EARLY NINETEENTH-CENTURY ENGRAVING shows St Mawes Castle, built near sea level on the harbour's eastern shore. In Henry VIII's time, four castles were planned but those at Gyllyngdune and on Trefusis Point were never built. Two castles were necessary to protect the harbour entrance because sixteenth-century artillery was so inaccurate at long range that Pendennis guns alone could not reach vessels entering the harbour on this side. The low-lying St Mawes Castle was indefensible from land attack and surrendered to Cromwell's army in 1646 without firing a shot although it is said that its treacherous governor delivered it to the enemy out of sympathy with their cause.

THE TWO ENGRAVINGS, above and to the right, look in opposite directions and show clearly the essentially waterside situation of Falmouth in its early days. Here the town is seen from the northern slopes of Pendennis towards the end of the eighteenth century. In the foreground, the part of the town known as the Bar, recently engulfed by modern development, was the site of many small, family-owned shipbuilding yards up to the 1920s. The tide mill, dating

THE VIEW ABOVE, seen from about the site of today's Claremont Terrace, looks towards Pendennis Point with Beacon Street, the main road into Falmouth until about 1800, in the foreground. Houses in those days were built of stone from local quarries and roofed with thatch or imported tiles. They were lit by candles or oil-lamps, and heated with coal or wood fires. Streets were very narrow. Disastrous house fires were common and hardly any of the town's buildings of this time have survived until today. In this waterside settlement, what is today the main shopping street was largely residential. Falmouth's other coast, looking south over the bay and the open sea, consisted of farmland running right down to the clifftop. Only during the mid-nineteenth century did building commence there.

(continued from previous page)
from Killigrew times, with the water-wheel on the end of mill building stands out clearly in the centre, its tidal mill pool on the near side of the mill, which was demolished as recently as 1914. Beyond the Bar stand the quays built by Peter Killigrew in 1670, marking the southern end of the town's narrow main street running past the church along the waterfront to Greenbank, the extent of which is wildly exaggerated on this print.

ARWENACK AVENUE, known to the Killigrews as the 'Long Walk', originally extended further south up the hill to meet Bar Lane (today's Melvill Road)at the upper end of what is now Lansdowne Road. At its northern end the tree-lined avenue had an impressive entrance, the gate-posts of which still stand as the only reminders of the old Arwenack Estate. The death of Martin Lister Killigrew in 1745 marked the end of the family name in Falmouth and it was not long before the new lord of the manor began to dispose of parts of the estate. The avenue was leased to Thomas Deeble in 1737 as a rope walk, a name by which it is still known to older residents, and Deeble's successors carried on this trade well into the nineteenth century. As the picture shows, a temporary form of roof was attached to the trees to give the workers some shelter. Beneath it, using imported hemp, the strands were stretched out over about eighty yards and twisted slowly to make the finished article, in great demand in a port such as Falmouth in the days of sailing ships. By 1900 the avenue had been restored to its original state with three rows of elm trees but a combination of pollution, vandalism and Dutch elm disease has left it a mere shadow of its former splendour.

Grove Place, Falmouth.

MARTIN LISTER KILLIGREW left Falmouth in 1725 and twelve years later wrote a series of letters to Abraham Hall, his successor as steward to the estate giving detailed instructions as to the size and method of construction of the Killigrew Monument, referring to it in one letter as a 'darling thing I am never to see'. His object in having it erected was never made clear and he insisted that there should be no inscription, not even a date. It was originally built in the centre of the Grove, an attractive park of elm trees immediately to the north of the manor house and on the site of the present Grove Place, seen in this picture as the terrace of three-storey houses. In 1836, when this part of the estate was sold for 'development', the monument was moved to the top of the hill at the extreme southern end of the Avenue (opposite) but in 1871, after houses had been erected there and the railway to Truro constructed, it stood precariously near a cutting and in the garden of Capt. Saulez RN, who objected to it. A second move took the monument to its present position on Arwenack Green, the site of the former semaphore station which had been pulled down about 1841. Here it stood in a small, fenced triangular park, surrounded by trees and close to the water's edge. Over a century later, it stands isolated from the sea by several stages of reclamation, in front of a rebuilt Arwenack House but boasting the plaque which its originator denied it.

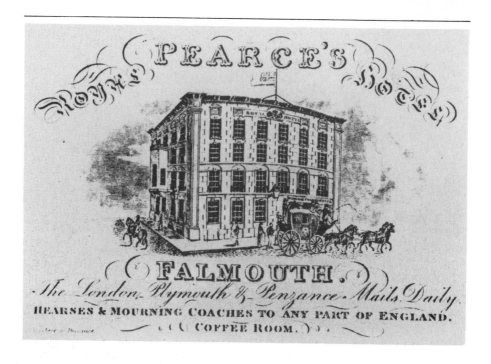

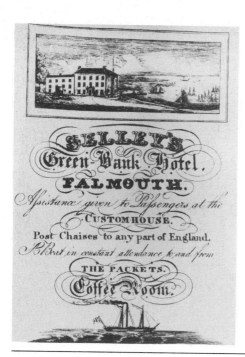

BOTH OF THESE HOTELS date from the days of the Packet Service. Pearce's Royal Hotel (above) was built for a consortium of packet captains wanting accommodation grand enough to match the elegance of their social life in the late eighteenth century. It became the town's main coaching inn and had stables, a smithy, and the town's first gasworks in the rear. Visitors must have found it somewhat disturbing that the Royal Mail coaches to London departed daily at 2.45 a.m. and the hotel's location next to the fish market was described in 1827 as 'a disgusting public nuisance'. Selley's Greenbank Hotel (below) is probably the oldest in the town to survive, dating from 1785. Its waterside position beside the King's Road, where the Packets lay at anchor before sailing, made it popular with passengers waiting to embark.

IN 1803 THE *LADY HOBART* PACKET, on the north Atlantic route to Halifax, Nova Scotia, struck an iceberg and sank after the crew had taken to the boats, as shown by this imaginative engraving of the incident. After this, winter sailings on the route were stopped.

BULK CARGOES OF GOLD were brought in on the Packets and carried to London in these large wagons, reminiscent of the American 'West', by Russell and Company, escorted by soldiers. Such a journey could take up to three weeks in bad weather and passengers who could not afford the coach travelled in them, walking most of the way by day and sleeping under them by night. Russell's headquarters stood at the bottom of Jacob's Ladder (p. 62) and when excavations were being dug for the new Lloyd's Bank, the old barred vaults in the hillside were uncovered. This is a reproduction of a framed picture purchased initially from John Burton's Old Curiosity Shop (p. 46) and now in the possession of Mr Ted Fisher.

MARLBOROUGH HOUSE was built in the early nineteenth century by Capt. John Bull on an estate to the west of the town and a carving of his Packet of the same name decorates the apex of the front wall. Furniture was brought from London and large numbers of trees, elm, beech, pine, Scotch fir and thorn (for hedging), shipped in by sea. The house stands today much as seen here, even to the garden walls, railings and urns but an extension has been added to each end of this historic building.

BELL'S COURT, at the end of an alley off Market Street, is best known as the location of the Packet Agent's office at the time of the Packet mutiny of 1810, where the magistrates read the Riot Act to the assembled, protesting Packet sailors. Today on this site a faithfully reconstructed building houses Falmouth's Maritime Museum.

THIS PAINTING BY J. CONDY, dating from 1851, shows a vessel believed to be HM Packet Brig *Crane* entering the harbour with St Mawes Castle in the background. Built at Woolwich Dockyard, probably in 1839, *Crane* was the ultimate in sailing Packet design and the only one of its kind to be constructed as steam vessels had already begun to take over the sailing routes. From 1839 to 1842 she sailed on the West Indies and Mexican station under Capt. John Hill, and between 1842 and 1850 to South America under first, Capt. Thomas A. Lewis, followed in 1847 by Capt. John Parsons. The outward sailing dates were in March and September and homeward dates, June/July and December/January. Her last sailing from Falmouth as a Packet was on 6 September 1850, and it is likely that this painting was commissioned to commemorate the final arrival of a sailing Packet in the port.

ARTHUR H. NORWAY, father of the successful novelist Nevil Shute (Norway), was an assistant secretary at the Post Office. One of his ancestors, John Arthur Norway, served with the Packet Service after having been invalided out of the Navy, and was killed in action in command of the Packet *Montagu* on 1 November 1813. His research into family history motivated him to write *The History of the Post Office Packet Service, 1793 to 1815*, published in 1895, after which the Royal Cornwall Polytechnic Society staged an exhibition of Packet memorabilia. The collective conscience of Falmouth people must have been aroused by his remarks about an almost total indifference towards the Service and, in 1897, a committee was formed 'for the purpose of raising a fund for the erection of a suitable monument to be placed in a public position in Falmouth . . .' to quote a fund-raising circular from its secretary, Revd W. Jago. Norway himself was not in favour of a monument but the plan went ahead and in November 1898, in what was described as 'a stirring scene' the memorial on the Moor was unveiled, as the picture shows. It was a granite obelisk 38 ft high, costing £300 and erected on a turf bank surrounded by railings. Susan Gay, in her book *Old Falmouth*, wrote of the ceremony, 'The Mayor and Corporation, clergy and officers of the navy and army, with detachments, were present, the town was bedecked with flags and a torpedo flotilla lay in the harbour, specially dispatched from Portland in honour of the occasion. A luncheon followed at the Municipal Buildings at which 100 guests were present; several old packetsmen stood in front of the monument and were likewise entertained.' The monument's inscription proclaims that it was, 'Erected by public subscription, AD 1898, to the memory of the gallant officers and men of HM Post Office Packet Service sailing from Falmouth, 1688–1852', and it is unfortunate that, after all their hard work, the committee got the final date wrong.

The Main Street

THE CONTINUOUS BUT FAR FROM STRAIGHT ROAD that runs alongside the Penryn River and Inner Harbour from Turnpike Creek to the docks — never more than forty yards from tidal water — has fifteen differently named sections. This is extremely puzzling for visitors, and new residents take some time to come to terms with these complexities of nomenclature; some never do! The northern part of the town, known as Penwerris, was in Budock parish until 1892 when it was incorporated into Falmouth Municipal Borough. At the time it was being developed as part of the expanding town of Falmouth the land was owned by Sir Francis Bassett, Baron de Dunstanville of Stratton, which explains some of the street names in the area. The church, pictured above, was built in 1828 to cater for the increasing population in this northern suburb, for the Pendennis garrison (which was then, and still is, in Budock ecclesiastical parish) and for the Packet crews, many of whom had settled here. The church was in the charge of a curate until July 1848, when Penwerris parish was created and it acquired its own vicar.

THIS VIEW SOUTHWARDS from outside the Greenbank Hotel dates from the 1890s and shows how much the waterfront has changed over the last 100 years. In the foreground are the workshops of Spear Brothers, coachbuilders, on the site previously occupied by Olver and Sons, builders, whose work in the district includes St Anthony lighthouse (1834/5) and the stations of the railway line to Truro (1862/3). Further along, by the Royal Cornwall Yacht Club, was the yard of coal merchants, John Pellow. This hotchpotch of buildings was cleared some years later to create Greenbank Gardens. Further south, the projection, known in those days as Pye's Cellars but more recently labelled Admiral's Quay by a recent developer, was a crowded residential area inhabited mostly by workers in the nearby maritime industries – shipwrights, boatmen, mariners and shipbuilders. On each side of the cellars was a boat-building yard – Thomas Jackett's Victoria Yard on the south and Thomas Gray's Well Yard on the north. Still further south, the densely built-up waterfront passes the Market Strand Pier, with a pleasure-boat alongside. The gasworks chimney and the parish church tower are in the far distance. Standing out clearly is the steep slope rising westwards along the entire waterfront, a feature which has created innumerable problems as Falmouth has spread inland.

AN EARLY TWENTIETH-CENTURY CARNIVAL PROCESSION has reached its turning point outside the Greenbank Hotel but there seems to be a hold up, probably along the narrow confines of Prince Street further along (p. 25). The high pavement on the right of the picture is characteristic of several Falmouth streets which have been built along a steep slope.

LOOKING IN THE OPPOSITE DIRECTION along Dunstanville Terrace from the high pavement, back towards the Greenbank Hotel. There are cows being driven along the road above the Royal Cornwall Yacht Club. Octavius Drew (known locally as 'Occy'), listed in the directories as 'livery stable proprietor and horse dealer', kept the cows in fields alongside Turnpike Creek and paid the local lads tuppence a week to fetch them to be milked in a shed just out of picture on the right. The ship's masts seen centre right probably belong to a coastal schooner unloading coal at Pellow's Yard.

AFTER THE ARRIVAL OF THE AUTOMOBILE, 'Occy' Drew's stables and cowshed were converted for use as a garage by J.J. Jane. On 19 July 1928, workmen on the beach below lit a bonfire which ignited the dry grass on the slope behind and flames spread rapidly to the garage. Employees tried to move the cars inside but when six had been saved, with two motor cycles and two pedal cycles, the smoke became so thick that they had to give up. Seven cars and one motor cycle were destroyed. 'Fair View House' adjoining the garage was badly damaged and its elderly occupants barely escaped with their lives. The engine of the Falmouth Fire Brigade (seen here) dealt with four large underground petrol tanks while the Truro Brigade pumped sea water onto the burning buildings in which petrol cans were exploding and flames rising twenty feet. Despite all these valiant efforts both garage and house were almost totally destroyed and a dangerously leaning wall had to be pulled down. Strangely, the Borough Council was negotiating to purchase these buildings with the aim of knocking them down for 'street improvements'. Within a year, J.J. Jane set up a new petrol station 200 yards along towards the town at the High Street junction with Beacon Street.

THE NARROW PRINCE STREET connects Dunstanville Terrace (known to most people today as Greenbank) with High Street. Among its original buildings were the Greenbank Dairy (p. 26), the Royal Oak public house and the large Congregational chapel which dominates the far end of this short street. Built in 1715 and enlarged in 1789, this old building was replaced in 1853 by a new chapel at the top of the High Street (p. 26), leaving this as a Sunday School. After all other buildings on that side of the street had been demolished in the 1890s the old chapel stood alone and became a distinct bottleneck for the increasing volume of traffic in the 1930s, especially the Penryn–Falmouth buses. It was eventually pulled down together with the whole of the opposite side of the street in the early 1950s. The road which disappears on the right of the picture past Winchester Buildings led by a roundabout route down to the waterfront where the two boatyards mentioned on p. 22 were located.

THE GREENBANK DAIRY, pictured here in the 1920s, stood nearly opposite the Congregational Sunday School. Even at this early date 'Cream by Post' was being advertised for the tourists. The reason for the photograph was that the shop window had been refashioned by a travelling window-dresser, and the Noall family pose for the picture. Other shops in Prince Street about this time were Baines, fruiterer and confectioner; Channon, baker; Jenkin, fruiterer; Martin, boot and shoe repairer; the Royal Oak public house; Barrett, fish and chip shop; and Penaluna, draper.

THE CONGREGATIONAL CHAPEL, opened in 1853, stands here between Jane's Garage and the Old Town Hall, itself a former Congregational chapel until replaced in 1715 by the, then, new building in Prince Street (p. 25). The farther building was bought by Martin Lister Killigrew and presented to the Corporation who used it as a Town Hall until it was replaced by a purpose-built home for municipal affairs on the Moor, in 1864.

THE TOP END OF HIGH STREET, known up to about sixty years ago by the alternative name of Ludgate Hill, shows much of the rebuilt west (right) side following the disastrous fire of 1862 (p. 28). The houses on the immediate left, including the pawnbroker's, were not destroyed in the fire and are among the oldest in the town today. George Eustice, stationer and newsagent, also ran a sub-post office while, further down, the tall building standing back from its neighbours has a sign advertising the 'National Cyclists Union' above the shop, for this was the Penwerris Temperance Hotel. In fact, the top seven shops on the right remain much the same today. Beyond them, the wall and gatepost show the location of Carne's Brewery Yard where the drays and horses were kept, together with all the stores, such as barrels, used in the brewery which stood until 1936 on the site of today's Tesco. In the far distance, on the left, it is interesting to notice that three of the stepped-down roof lines have survived the 1862 fire and stand out clearly beyond the devastation shown on p. 28. Photographs of this period always seem to have evoked great interest from passers-by who are only too willing to stand and provide the local colour, without which such pictures would be far less interesting.

'ON THE MORNING OF SATURDAY, THE 12TH OF APRIL, 1862, the largest and most calamitous fire that probably ever visited the County of Cornwall took place at Falmouth. Its site was in the High Street, a steep hill leading out of the town . . . the street running nearly north and south and being extremely narrow. The houses in this locality were mostly very old, many of them built of partition work and in several ways were readily disposed to ignite and burn fiercely. The conflagration began about 1 a.m. and continued unchecked until nearly 6 a.m. causing the destruction of about 30 houses and £30,000 worth of property.' So begins the story of the High Street fire, written in booklet form and published by Fred. H. Earle, a printer on the Quay. It probably began in a defective chimney in the tenements to the rear of Mr Rawlings' grocery shop, beside Briton's Court, and spread rapidly to destroy Barnett's photographers, next door. Bursting through Rawlings' window, the flames leapt across the narrow street to Dinnis's spirit store and in the strong easterly wind continued up both sides of the hill to destroy the shops of thirteen traders, many of whom were uninsured. Thirty residential properties, houses and tenements, were also destroyed together with many sheds and outhouses. The alarm was raised by PC Prater of the Borough Constabulary who organized a supply of water from a hose attached to a fire-plug outside Dinnis's shop, installed for that very purpose by the Waterworks Company when the main was laid in 1848. Later, a powerful engine arrived from the castle garrison, manned by artillerymen, and this was soon joined by an engine landed from HMS *Russell* and two engines from Penryn. Their total efforts were largely ineffective and the premises of seven traders at both ends of the fire had to be demolished to prevent its spreading further. The decision to create these firebreaks was made after consultation between the Mayor (J. Olver), Capt. Hall of HMS *Russell* and Lieut. Thomas of the castle garrison. Special commendation was made to the Borough Police, especially PC Richards for his 'indomitable zeal', the sailors and soldiers 'who showed somewhat of the gallantry in the face of danger which British soldiers are famed for' and, among many others, Mr T. Lanyon, currier, 'whose brawny arms were bared to the work', and Mr P.H. Pearson who 'wielded the axe to good purpose on the roofs of the houses demolished'.

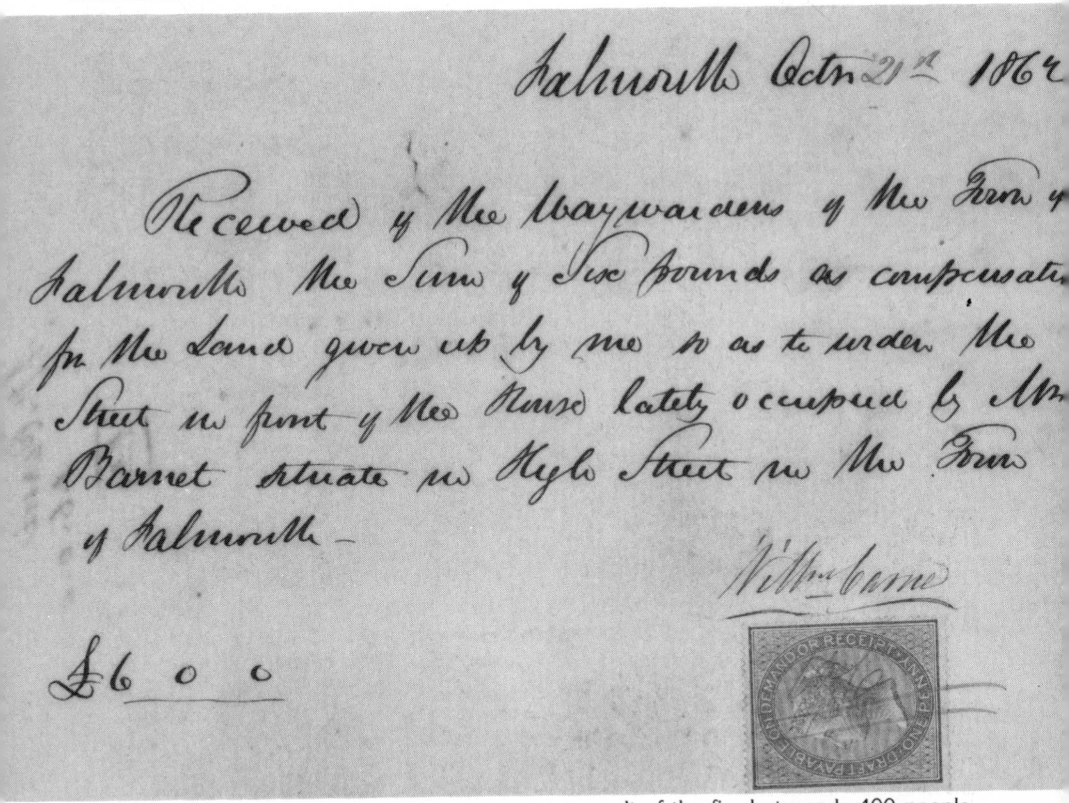

Falmouth October 21st 1864

Received of the Waywardens of the Town of Falmouth the Sum of Six pounds as compensation for the land given up by me so as to widen the Street in front of the House lately occupied by Mr Barnet situate in Kyle Street in the Town of Falmouth —

£6 0 0

William Carne

AMAZINGLY THERE WERE NO SERIOUS CASUALTIES as a result of the fire but nearly 400 people were rendered homeless, mostly 'labouring men and their families'. Relief measures were swift and effective. Money was subscribed to a fund and over £500 was soon raised; clothing was collected and meals prepared daily at the Polytechnic Hall. Accommodation was offered in many parts of the town — the National School, the British School, a large house in Porhan Street belonging to Lord Wodehouse as well as space in many private houses. Reconstruction of the damage took some years to complete and it was decided to widen the High Street by ten feet in the process. How narrow the street was before the fire can be seen clearly in the picture opposite. Responsibility for all things to do with the highways in the Borough lay in the hands of the Waywardens (sometimes called Surveyors of the Highways), elected members of the Borough Council who were, in turn, elected by their fellow councillors to do the job for a year. It was not a popular appointment but the only two reasons for refusing it were death or residence outside the Borough... and some prospective candidates did actually move house to avoid having to fill the post. The illustration above shows a receipt issued to the Waywardens by William Carne, the property owner, for a strip of land in front of what had been Barnett's photographers shop, for road widening. Whenever I walk up the High Street, I find it difficult to visualize it ten feet narrower than it is today.

THIS PICTURE OF THE LOWER END OF HIGH STREET dates from between 1906, when Lipton's took over the premises in the distance – formerly the Capital and Counties' Bank – and 1911, when the buildings on the right, below Knowles, butcher, were demolished. Their rough frontage of local stone, and small panes of glass in the shop windows, suggest they were very old and could possibly date from the late eighteenth century. Once they had been knocked down to widen the street, Nos 24 and 25 disappeared from the High Street. This part was not affected by the fire and both road and granite pavement were very narrow, although part of the pavement in this vicinity is no wider today.

THE SITE OF THE HUMBLE HAMLET OF SMITHICK from which, in time, the early town spread along the waterfront in both directions. In those early days a creek ran up to the road on the near side of the King's Hotel, its narrow beach or 'strand' exposed at low tide. To its right, a marsh stretched up the valley that was to become known as the Moor and between creek and marsh ran the road to Arwenack Manor, as shown on an old map of 1613. The right to hold a market was granted to Peter Killigrew (I) in 1652 and the first market house was probably built where the shops in the right foreground stand; hence the name of this short stretch of road is Market Strand.

THIS MAY BE ONE OF THE EARLIEST PHOTOGRAPHS to have been taken in Falmouth, dating as it does from 1863 and showing the departure from the Market Strand of the last stagecoach; the railway had arrived. Before 1797, all mail for the Packets arrived on horseback, direct from London: most passengers arrived by sea as land travel was both arduous and dangerous. As the roads slowly improved, mail coaches reached Falmouth bringing some passengers, although the journey was far from enjoyable, especially in bad weather.

ONE OF SEVERAL BACK-ALLEYS in the rear of the main street is Bakehouse Yard, connecting Webber Street with Market Strand. Its name is probably derived from the fact that in this confined space, two bakers, Richard D. Rolling and A.E. Webber, baked their bread. Rolling's shop is probably the one on the right with the bow window.

SIMMONS' KING'S ARMS HOTEL was demolished in 1902/3 to make way for the King's Hotel, seen on p. 31. It may have been the oldest tavern in the town as it is mentioned in what has become known as the Falmouth Manuscript written by Martin Lister Killigrew in 1738. For a short time between 1809 and 1817 the name was used by one of its former waiters who had taken over and renamed the Greenbank Hotel while this establishment, as seemed to be the fashion at that time, was known as Commins' Hotel after its owner. Towards the end of its life, this hotel became rather shabby and run-down and a newspaper report in the 1890s said that its main customers were farmers on market days, and sailors and boatmen, who used the 'tap' as the public bar was then called. On the extreme right, the newly-built Capital and Counties' Bank with its bold granite façade has replaced the older shops shown on p. 39.

AS THE TOWN OF FALMOUTH began to develop along the waterfront, Smithick Creek was built up with sea walls and it became the main landing place at this end of the town. In this picture, a trading ketch lies on the beach at low water. Eventually a stone pier or landing place was constructed here.

PRESSURE FOR A MORE SUBSTANTIAL LANDING PLACE at Market Strand became so great that in 1871 the Corporation constructed the Market Strand Pier (pp. 112–13) at a cost of £1,732. This granite structure filled in the former basin, shown opposite, and stretched well out into the harbour with a projection on the north side equipped with a hand-operated crane. Within thirty years this had become inadequate for the larger, deeper vessels wanting to use it so it was extended further. The inland section became, as the photograph shows, one of the town's four main cab ranks and three of the horse-drawn vehicles stand waiting for custom. The flat-roofed building on the right is a pumping station for the town's sewerage system.

VIEWED FROM THE END OF MARKET STREET, this photograph shows the Market Strand and the lower end of High Street. The three step-roofed buildings which survived the 1862 fire stand out clearly on the right of High Street. The demolition of the old buildings opposite them (p. 30) had not yet taken place and the large hoarding advertising the Duke of Cornwall Hotel is attached to them. The impressive entrance to the recently-erected King's Hotel faces a row of shops which, from the far end, were: Gilbert's Queen's Arms public house; Theophilus Jones, tobacconist; Henry Liddicoat, grocer and wine and spirit merchant (on the site of the former Market House); Albert Edward Webber, grocer and restaurateur; Star Tea Company Limited, confectioner, pastrycook and biscuit manufacturer, wholesale and retail corn and flour factor; and Osborne, grocer.

FALMOUTH FROM HARBOUR TERR.

BEFORE ENTERING MARKET STREET, it is interesting to look at the town's main shopping area in this photograph dating from the 1890s, taken from the elevated viewpoint of Erisey Terrace. On the left is the Market Strand with its landing place in the break in the buildings. The bold advertisement for 'Grose's General Drapery Emporium and Carpet Warehouse' marks the narrow bend at the beginning of Market Street, forced upon the early builders by a spur of high ground projecting towards the harbour from Porhan Hill. As the street then turns to follow the line of the waterfront, the large roof of the old Baptist Church stands out and, behind it, houses in Smithick Hill rise along the steep slope, overlooked by Vernon Place. In the distance, Pendennis headland rises to the castle on its flat top with the early docks jetties in its shelter. To its right the low isthmus with the square Falmouth Hotel marks the open sea coast.

A COMPARISON OF THIS 1860S SKETCH with the picture on the opposite page shows how great an obstruction Bassett, Grocer must have been at the entrance to Market Street even in the days of horse-drawn traffic. The building stretched halfway across the road towards Truscott, Butcher, and an old newpaper reported that on one occasion the lifeboat got stuck there and had to be taken back. In May 1877 a deputation led by the mayor, Mr T. Webber, asked Lord Kimberley to remove this building to ease congestion in the street and after some negotiation, it was demolished. Between Bassett's and the King's Arms a road led in on the left to the hotel stables. The shop shown as Truscott's on the opposite page was, in these days, the Victory Inn, kept by Mrs Catherine Pascoe and the Kimberley Inn, next door, was kept by Mrs Allen who had a brewery further up Killigrew Street. The shops on the right, from the far end, were Bennett, grocer; Gutheridge, draper; Lanyon, currier; and Webber, restaurant.

THIS 1902 VIEW of the north end of Market Street shows several differences from later pictures of the area. Although Truscott's, butcher, remained well into this century, Hawke, boot and shoe maker, was soon to be demolished to make way for the new Capital and Counties' Bank, by 1910 converted to Lipton's grocery store with the Café Royal upstairs (clearly named on p. 31). Further along, John Palmer, general and fancy goods merchants, and Henry L. Owen, watchmaker and jeweller, stood before the bottom of Smithick Hill. The premises facing the viewer are, on the right, Rowe and Corlyon, auctioneers, with offices above for J.R. Corlyon, accountant and permanent secretary to the Oddfellows; next on the left is the four-storey furniture warehouse of J. Grose and Son. On the opposite side of the road is parked one of Cyrus Best's horse-buses, waiting for passengers. His stables in Gyllyng Street have only recently been demolished to make way for housing.

THE OLD ESTABLISHED FIRM of Downing and Son (1779) had this large drapery and dressmaking emporium at London House until it was taken over by Cox and Horder just before the First World War. A customer's carriage waits outside. No double yellow lines in those days!

AT THE NARROW PART OF MARKET STREET, Grose's and the adjoining two shops appear to be empty, awaiting demolition. They had been occupied by F. Hosking MPS, dispensing family chemist, and F. Andrews, baker and pastrycook. All three premises were replaced in 1937 by the more modern building of Montague Burton, tailor and outfitter.

THE BAPTIST MOVEMENT is the oldest nonconformist group in Falmouth, dating from the Civil War when many of the Commonwealth soldiers were of this persuasion. After the Restoration, despite the persecution which followed, a Baptist Society was formed locally but their first Meeting House was not built in the town until 1769; its whereabouts is not known. In 1778 a malt house at the top of Well Lane was taken over and converted into a chapel at a cost of £146 17s. 9d., and this was followed by a purpose-built chapel in Saffron Court, off Webber Street, in 1804, enlarged in 1806. Increases in the size of the congregation led to the chapel pictured above being built between 1875 and 1877 on the site of Roskilly's timber-yard and carpenter's shop. Costing £55,000 and erected by local builder, J.W. Halligey, its members chose to call it Emmanuel. The former Bible Christian chapel on Smithick or 'Back' Hill was bought as a Sunday School and also used as a soup kitchen. By 1939, the chapel had become too large for its congregation and, as the site in the main street was so valuable, it was sold and a new church built on Western Terrace.

THE MARKET STREET FIRE of Sunday 5 January 1870, was as destructive as the High Street fire of eight years before, but in this case only one side of the street was destroyed; shop-fronts on the opposite side were badly scorched but no properties were lost. The blaze probably began in a store behind the shops, but by the time it was discovered the building was alight and the fire spreading. As was so often the case, the water supply from the town's fire-cocks was totally inadequate and the Falmouth Volunteer Fire Brigade could make little impression with their hand-pump. Assistance was summoned from Penryn, whose brigade ran a hose down to the sea for water, while men from HMS *Ganges* attacked the fire from the seaward side using a pump mounted on a boat, despite the danger caused by paraffin, thrown from Fox's ironmonger's store, catching fire on the surface of the water. Eventually the fire was controlled but not before several shops and houses had been totally destroyed, including Carne, brewer; Geach, draper; Kelway and Osborn, grocers; Turner, tailor; Goodman, currier; Curtis' eating house; Johns, boots and shoes; Fox, ironmonger; and Rundell, grocer. The picture shows the extent of the destruction but the frontage of the County Police Station (see p. 44) somehow survived, although the rear of the building was badly damaged. Reconstruction took several years and property owners were paid to allow the new buildings to be set back six feet from their original line.

MARKET STREET IN THE EARLY TWENTIETH CENTURY, showing the impressive reconstruction following the fire. Wearne, watchmaker and jeweller, Oliver, boots and shoes, and Carver, watchmaker and jeweller retain their original frontages but the County Police Station has given way to Goodings, ladies' and gents' tailor, who have expanded from the shop next door, the nearest of the new buildings. Above Goodings are Charles Everett, dental surgeon, and Reginald Rogers, solicitors, commissioners for oaths, clerk to the commissioners of taxes, and clerk to the Guardians. Between Olivers and Carvers was a passage leading to one of the many residential areas found behind the shops in the main street, this one known as Renfree's Yard. Further along, several family businesses have become established, including Spooner's 'Bon Marché', drapers and outfitters; R.C. Clarke and Co, tailors and hatters, and Gedny's drapers. Once again, a group of interested passers-by pose for the camera. The absence of any kind of wheeled vehicle contrasts sharply with the situation along this stretch of road today.

IN THIS BUILDING, which survived the 1870 fire, the distinctive bay windows of the County Police Station show clearly. When the new station was built in Berkeley Vale in 1901, as shown on p. 66, this building became a shop and the windows disappeared in the new shop-front. There had been two police stations in Market Street, but the Borough Police were disbanded in the early 1890s when all policing in the Borough was handed over to the County Constabulary.

THE CURVING FRONTAGE OF THE ROYAL HOTEL remained like this up to the 1920s when reconstruction took place and the whole façade was moved back several feet to reduce the sharp angle into Church Street. The rebuilt hotel had only three storeys but the attractive wrought-iron balconies were retained and the overall shape of the building faithfully reproduced. The Central Supply Stores stood at the top of the Fish Strand, and the fish market of ill repute was opposite, next to the hotel. The rectangular space on the hotel's ground floor led to the hotel entrance and, after 1928, to the Grand Theatre, built by Harris Brothers; it was demolished in the mid-1980s.

JOHN BURTON came to Falmouth in 1862 and began business with a 'cloam' (earthenware) stall in the market. Eventually he settled at 27 Market Street where, for twenty-five years, he conducted a most unorthodox business in curios and oddities in his world famous Old Curiosity Shop. He formulated a set of rules for living 100 years, among which were: sleep on your right side; do not have your bedstead against the wall; eat little meat and see that it is well cooked; eat plenty of fat to feed the cells which destroy disease germs; avoid tea but take plenty of cocoa and chocolate; watch the three Ds – drinking water, damp and drains. His shop was full of exotic objects obtained through his many contacts locally and among ships' crews visiting the port. On one occasion he bought the Penryn Borough stocks in which a couple of his croneys were frequently photographed, usually outside public houses. After uproar in the 'ancient Borough' he offered to return them if some Penryn councillors would sit in them, and when this offer was refused he sold them to someone else. He also

tried to buy the old Eddystone lighthouse (Smeaton's Tower) for £500 but indignant protests from irate Plymothians persuaded Trinity House to keep it in Plymouth for erection on the Hoe. In 1884, at the famous cannibalism trial at the Old Town Hall, he put up the bail of £1,000 for the three defendants. When the Prince of Wales visited Falmouth in 1887, he sent a message to Burton asking that some of his 'objects' be sent to him for inspection; to which J.B. replied, politely, that if 'respected Albert Edward' wanted to see them, he should come to the shop! He died in 1907 and the business passed to his oldest son, Tom, who carried it on into the 1930s but lacked the paternal flair for publicity.

THESE OLD SHOPS – Maunder's Refreshment Rooms, Trevarthe, baker, Collins, grocer – stood in Church Street in the 1890s but they were demolished in June 1905 to widen the pavement. On the extreme left is the entrance to Somercourt, another residential area behind the main street shops, with houses occupied by two labourers, a chimney sweep, two shipwrights and three mariners. The gas lamp attached to the corner of Maunder's was one of over thirty in the streets of the town, supplied from the gasworks opposite. The Borough Corporation was continually in dispute with the gas company over the quality of its gas, the blacking of the glasses around the mantles by impurities with the consequent loss of illumination, and their constant digging up of the street. In some ways, time changes little!

NEXT TO HICK'S GLASS AND CHINA WAREHOUSE stood this impressive building with six columns and railings housing the Falmouth Subscription Rooms, founded in 1826. Consisting of a spacious news and reading room, two billiards rooms (upstairs), a smoking room and a committee room, this institution was founded by the town's business men as a convivial meeting place. Officers of the Navy and the Army, together with 'all respectable strangers' who visited the port had the privilege of free admission. In the reading room was kept a backlog of newspapers so that returning ships' officers could catch up with the news. As Philp's Panorama of Falmouth (1827) states '. . . here amusement blended with intelligence is at hand at all hours, and the opportunity of conversation and acquaintance with respectable men . . .', adding 'as a further recommendation, in the evening, brilliantly lighted with gas.' By 1914 its name had changed to the Falmouth Club and in the early 1920s this moved to a new location at the former Falmouth Tennis Club on Western Terrace. This building was converted into two shops, which necessitated the installation of shop-fronts behind the pillars, two of which were removed for the shops' doorways. The upper storey was extended over the pillars and converted to living accommodation.

ONE OF THE LARGEST of the town's residential enclaves behind the shops in the main street was Snow's Court, entered through a narrow passage between the properties of Brima-combe, painter and glazier, and Elizabeth Notwill, grocer. Rising towards the end of the cobbled court with its granite-lined gutters were nineteen working-class houses, as well as Brimacombe's paint workshop and J.H. Peters' bakehouse. They were all demolished in 1912 to make way for the St George's Cinema, built by Harris Brothers, whose monogram still decorates the ornate frontage. This was Falmouth's first purpose-built cinema although other halls had previously been used for this novel and increasingly popular form of entertainment of which the Harrises seem to have established something of a monopoly. The St George's was said to accommodate 1,100 people and, in a booklet issued to celebrate its opening, its owners described it as 'an imposing, substantial, ornate structure of brick and stone with fireproof floors . . . The front elevation is executed in freestone from the Bath Stone Quarries and is of the Renaissance period.' Inside 'the decorations of the hall will surprise all who enter for the first time. The finely moulded, elliptical ceiling is supported by fluted doric columns . . . and in the panels round the sides of the hall are rich tapestries representing various scenes'. In the 1950s the cinema was burnt down and replaced, a few years later, by a shopping arcade which not only retained the name but, happily, also the decorative frontage.

THE ROYAL CORNWALL POLYTECHNIC SOCIETY was founded in 1833 by Anna-Maria and Caroline, the two teenage daughters of Robert Were Fox. As Quakers, they were concerned about the well-being of the working classes and, under father's guidance, sought to create a means by which the artisans of the Perran Foundry could exhibit their ideas and inventions to a wider public and, in founding the Society, became the first in Britain to use the word 'Polytechnic', meaning 'of many arts or techniques'. In 1834/5 this building was constructed with a large hall to stage exhibitions (p. 52) while the rooms at the front housed the Public Dispensary, Savings Bank and Subscription Library.

THE POLYTECHNIC HALL, was used for a wide range of activities, and here the Falmouth Volunteer Fire Brigade is holding a fund-raising bazaar. The sign invites the public to the 'Haunt of the Mermaids'. In those days such organizations as the Fire Brigade were largely financially self-supporting, with little help from the local authority. A comparison with the above photographs shows that the post office next door has been built, dating this picture after 1872.

THE MAIN EVENT in the calendar of the Royal Cornwall Polytechnic Society was its Annual Exhibition and here, in the hall, is the impressive assembly of speakers, organizers and exhibitors at the 50th Jubilee Exhibition of 1882. Among the few ladies present is the Society's co-founder, Miss Anna-Maria Fox, seated to the left of the table between the bearded gentleman and the lamp. Exhibitions such as this were a means by which changes could be made in mining technology with a view to improving the working conditions of the miners. By offering prizes, called 'premiums', good ideas were presented to mine owners and in this way, the Society was responsible for introducing such life-saving innovations as the safety fuse, new types of explosive, ventilation of mines, wire rope, rock drilling and, perhaps most beneficial of all, the 'man-engine', designed to replace the dangerous ladders attached to the walls of the shaft.

THIS IMPRESSIVE POST OFFICE was built in 1872 on the initiative of twenty of the town's leading businessmen who paid for its construction. Before this, the post office had been located wherever the Postmaster decided and over the years had moved at least eight times. Inadequate accommodation had led to inefficiency and late deliveries so the businessmen had each bought between one and five shares to a total of forty, each worth £50. Furthermore, the post office had recently taken over the operation of the electric telegraph in 1869, and this revolutionary means of communication needed to be better housed as the Falmouth office dealt with many overseas calls. In 1871 it had been reported in a local newspaper that messages to the Far East now took up to four hours, compared with several months by sea prior to the invention of the electric telegraph and the laying of submarine cables.

THIS GROUP OF POST OFFICE WORKERS pictured outside the Polytechnic Hall in 1908 with their horse-drawn van were recorded by Mr C.A. 'Charlie' Symonds, himself a postman and an inveterate photographer of local scenes and subjects, to whom we should be eternally grateful for having given us so many interesting details of everyday life in Falmouth around the turn of the century. In this photograph are, left to right, Mr W.J. Price, Assistant Inspector; Walter Williams, postman; Mr Peters, postman, and Mr Butland, driver. Mr Price, a well-known local historian, worked at Falmouth post office for forty-five years, starting as a telegraph messenger boy in 1880, in which capacity he delivered the first message received at Falmouth by the Direct Spanish Telegraph Company's cable from the burgomaster at Bilbao to the Mayor of Falmouth, Mr J.C. Downing. He became an established postman in 1885 when he earned £1 per week for an eleven hour day. He retired in 1925 as Assistant Inspector.

THE DOUBLE BEND IN THE MAIN STREET known as Church Corner results from the existence in the early days of a creek round which the original cliff-top path had to go. In this photograph the cab rank with its six cabs and their drivers pose for the camera, accompanied by a policeman and a group of interested spectators. There were five cab proprietors, most of whom are probably represented here, although one of them, Aaron Smith, had his offices to the left of the picture and may have taken priority on this rank; his stables were at the town end of Avenue Road. The others were Simon Gay, with stables in New Street mews (now Brook Place); Cyrus Best of Gyllyng Street; George Rowe, behind the Royal Hotel; and Octavius Drew of Greenbank. The cabmen's shelter is to the right of the rank behind which one of the parish church windows is just visible. The photograph was taken before 1925 when the Church Institute was built in the grassy, shrub-covered area at the far end of the rank.

806A. Parish Church, Falmouth, w.m.h.

DURING THE CIVIL WAR Pendennis Castle had given shelter to Henrietta Maria, Queen of Charles I in 1644, and to the Prince of Wales, later Charles II, on his way into exile two years later. While in Pendennis, Prince Charles promised that the town should have a church and after the Restoration he granted a Charter and helped to pay for the church, which was dedicated to his father, King Charles the Martyr. Building was begun in 1662 and the church consecrated in 1665, but that structure was very different from the fine edifice seen today; originally smaller and with a shorter tower, built in 1684, additions and alterations were made regularly. A chancel was added in 1684, galleries between 1686 and 1703, as shown in the photograph, and the tower was raised for a clock in 1800, when battlements were added. In the early nineteenth century both the fabric and the spiritual condition of the church seem to have reached a low ebb before, in 1830, the advowson, or the right to nominate a successor to a vacant benefice, was bought by General Coope who installed his son, William John, to the living in 1838. The next thirty-two years were those of spiritual controversy and improvement to the building. When Revd Coope arrived the church was in a poor state of repair with rotting floors, leaking windows, collapsing roof and an unsafe tower; he rectified all these and made many improvements including a new pulpit and greatly improved lighting.

UNFORTUNATELY, COOPE'S IMPROVEMENTS WERE NOT LONG LASTING and by 1896, during the incumbency of another hard working but far less controversial rector, Brian Christopherson, the church was almost completely rebuilt. The photograph shows the east wall and part of the south wall with the round granite pillars haphazardly spread about the rubble-strewn floor. The walls were made higher, a new roof added and new moulded ceilings put in. Two new columns were built in the choir, the north and south galleries (shown opposite) were removed and the west gallery renewed. But, as is often the case in such operations, shortage of money prevented many proposed improvements such as a new organ chamber, new tower and a new south entrance, although these were subsequently made when money became available. The tower was re-roofed in 1906, electric lighting was switched on in November 1907, and for these and other good works Christopherson was made a Freeman of the Borough (see p. 125). More recently, in 1967, probably because of percolating water, some granite pillars were given new foundations and the result of all these structural works has been to give Falmouth a fine parish church with much of the town's history depicted in its wall plaques and memorials.

THE CUSTOM HOUSE, with its impressive Doric columns and finely-coloured Georgian coat-of-arms, stands at the southern end of Arwenack Street, its rear on the quay which shares its name. In 1650 Peter Killigrew persuaded the Commonwealth authorities to establish a Custom House in the growing settlement and gave land for its construction in what became Mulberry Square, beside Smithick Creek and near the bottom of Ludgate Hill.

By the late eighteenth century the focus of trade had moved to the Killigrew quays and for convenience the Custom House was moved to what is now 2 Bank Place which, in turn, became too small with expanding trade and increased Packet activity, so that this building was erected in 1814. Behind it, on the Quay, is the Queen's (King's) Pipe, thought to date from the earliest years of this building and used for burning contraband goods. The lower picture shows Arwenack Street and the Custom House decorated for the Coronation of King Edward VII in 1903.

THAT PART OF THE HARBOUR SHORE immediately south of the quays became known as the 'Bank' and when Robert Were Fox built a new house there in 1788 he called it Bank House. It is said that although he planned the house he did not enter it until it was completed and the key handed to him. It became a happy family house for several generations of Foxes and after Robert Were died in 1848 his grandson, Robert Barclay Fox and his wife lived there for a short time before moving to Penjerrick. In 1864 the lease was sold to Mr John Downing who used the north end as a biscuit factory while his son, a coal merchant, used the basement and yard for storing coal. In 1868 a fire swept through the building and the roof fell in, but so solidly had the house been built that the walls were intact and when the interior had been rebuilt and the building re-roofed it became the Bank House Hotel until taken over by the YMCA in the early 1930s.

THIS YACHT stands on what was the Grove Place beach until dumping of waste material from dock extensions in the late 1920s and early 1930s obliterated it. The terrace of houses behind it was originally built as private residences for the well-off in the 1840s but by the time of the photograph were occupied by doctors' surgeries, a hairdressing establishment, three hotels and the Girls' Friendly Society.

ONLY THE LARGE HOUSE CALLED 'PENWENNACK' at the far end of Bar Terrace had been built in 1864. By 1890 the thirty-two houses stood as seen here, most of them occupied by workers in the shipyards on the Bar opposite or in the dockyard further along the road.

The Moor

THE MOOR, regarded by most Falmothians as the town centre, was originally a marshy area bordering the stream flowing into Smithick Creek and bounded on each side by steeply rising hills. Only after the town was well established along the waterfront did growth begin in this area and no road had been built up this valley as a way out of the main street until the early nineteenth century. Once the marsh had been drained sufficiently, expansion here was rapid and, by 1827, Killigrew Street and Berkeley Place were developing. In this early twentieth-century photograph the Moor is well established as an open space with the Packet Memorial surrounded by some of the town's principal buildings.

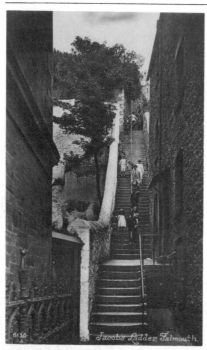

Left:

JACOB'S LADDER, with 111 steps, installed in the 1830s or '40s, has no biblical association. Jacob Hamblen, builder, tallow-chandler and property owner built it to facilitate communication between his business – at the bottom – and some of his property at the top. The building at the bottom right was once the office of Russell's haulage business, responsible for conveying to London gold brought in on the Packets (see p. 17).

(see p. 17)

Below:

JOHN WESLEY FIRST VISITED FALMOUTH in 1745 when, in his own words, he was taken prisoner by an immense mob 'gaping and roaring like lions'. His later visits were far more peaceful but it was only in 1754 that Methodism was established in Falmouth. Their first chapel was probably in Porhan Street but in 1791, the year of Wesley's death, this chapel was built on the south side of the Moor and, as its congregation increased, was enlarged in 1814.

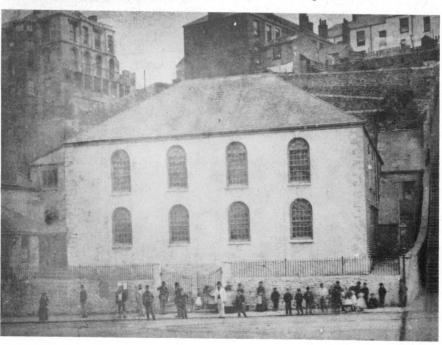

THIS LATE-NINETEENTH-CENTURY VIEW of the south side of the Moor, before the Packet Memorial had been erected, presents an entirely different picture from that of today. Dominating the scene is the Methodist church, built to replace that shown opposite in 1876. It was bombed twice during the Second World War, in October 1940 and May 1941, when there were casualties among members of HM Forces and local church people as the building was in use as a Forces' canteen. The exterior changed little following its reconstruction in 1956. The white building may have been built as the short-lived Catholic and Apostolic church (Irvingites) but this closed in 1863. It was reopened, probably in1876, as a Mission church but was largely replaced when the much larger All Saints' Church opened at the top of Killigrew Street in 1890. Next door is the Foresters Arms, later renamed the Wodehouse Inn. Apart from the general sense of openness in this picture, probably the most striking difference is that most of the properties shown are residential; there are very few shops, and the three shown are, from the Mission church down, Richard Tregunna, fancy dealer; Faithful Veale, tailor, and Miss Lydia P. Mitchell, butcher. Today the ground floors of all these buildings have been taken over as shops but their upper storeys remain much the same.

THE CLASSICAL AND MATHEMATICAL SCHOOL was founded in 1825 in this building in Killigrew Street. Within five years the school had closed as a result of financial problems but soon reopened following drastic reorganization. Renamed Falmouth Grammar School, it became an accepted part of the town's educational structure until 1894 when it really prospered under the headmastership of Mr Newland Deakin. He was responsible for building the Boarding House (now the Melvill Hotel), seen below, and after the Education Act of 1902 made local authorities responsible for secondary education, supervised the move to new premises in Quarter Mile Lane (now Tregenver Road) in 1914. This building survived as a Day Continuation School and the District Education Offices for many years until demolished in the 1950s to make way for Falmouth Technical College.

HERE, THE SALVATION ARMY BAND leads a group of French fishermen, stormbound in the harbour, across the Moor past the Packet Memorial in February 1925. Beside the Memorial stands a tank from the First World War brought to the town with great ceremony a few years earlier (see p. 133). 'Army surplus' equipment was liberally disposed of in this way and, in addition to the tank, there were guns along the sea front, on Pendennis Point and in Kimberley Park.

ANOTHER 1920S PHOTOGRAPH OF THE MOOR shows a fair in full swing on what was then the Market Place; the roof of the Market House, by now largely derelict, is in the foreground. There were protests over the presence of the fair from some residents and councillors but this was countered by other residents who said they liked it and did not object to it. The compromise was to move it to the top part of the Moor in later years.

NOWHERE IS THE CONTRAST BETWEEN PAST AND PRESENT more vividly seen than in these two pictures in which the upper Moor is shown as a quiet open space. The photograph above is dominated by the impressive new County Police Station built in 1901 at the lower end of Berkeley Vale, next to the widened Quarry Hill. Below this, Berkeley Place – it is sad that this name has gone out of use today – is largely residential. Below, members of the rugby club are photographed before setting out in four charabancs for an excursion in 1922; rugby 'caps' are worn by several players. In the background the four cottages in Cross Row, demolished in 1937, and the abundance of trees give this view an almost rural appearance.

THE LOWER END OF BERKELEY PLACE, originally made up of three-storey houses as seen above, was transformed in 1933 when, with the construction of the modern building seen below, it became known as Co-op Corner. The Falmouth Co-operative Society Limited had been in business at 18 Arwenack Street but increased trade prompted a move to these larger, better sited premises. In the following years other buildings in Berkeley Place were taken over by the Co-op, but they were all vacated in the 1980s when the Leo's superstore was built at Ashfield to qualify easily as the town's most hideous structure, its exterior covered with plastic 'carbuncles'.

THE MARKET HOUSE was built on the Moor in 1812/13, on land belonging to Lord Wodehouse, to replace the original structure in Market Strand which had not only become too small, but its foundations were insecure. This photograph shows a gathering in the Market Place on the occasion of a visit by the Prince of Wales (later Edward VII) on 2 November 1887 to lay the foundation stone of All Saints' Church, taking advantage of a visit to the county to lay the foundation stone of Truro Cathedral. Inside the Market House can be seen the roofed fountain which still stands on the Moor while, on the slope above, are, from left to right: Trevethan Hall, bought by John Burton in 1895 and demolished to make way for Mount Edgcumbe Terrace; Trevethan Board School, built in 1877; and, lower down, the New Market Inn, access to the back yard of which was gained by means of a tunnel whose entrance is seen in the wall below the Inn. The sloping path, in this picture lined with spectators, is still called Board School Hill by older residents. On the skyline above Erisey Terrace is Belle Vue Terrace (later, Trevethan Road) with, at its left end, the Cornwall Home for Destitute Little Girls, built in 1871 on land given by the lord of the manor, Lord Kimberley, costing £900, and accommodating thirty 'inmates'. In 1929 the Market House was sold to Harris Brothers as a site for a theatre but they, in turn, sold it to the government who built a new Post Office and Telephone Exchange.

TOWARDS THE END OF THE NINETEENTH CENTURY, with increasing educational provision, more people were learning to read . . . but what were they to read? The answer came in the form of libraries. There had been a subscription library in the Polytechnic Society building since the 1830s, and many of the town's booksellers and stationers had small libraries as a sideline, but the reading explosion demanded free libraries. The Borough Corporation agonized over this for several years as it involved spending ratepayers' money, but eventually their reluctance to do anything about it persuaded philanthropist, Mr John Passmore Edwards, who had already donated a hospital to the town (see p. 157) in 1893 and was given the Freedom of the Borough as a result, to give them enough money to build a library. There was some debate over the site but eventually the cheapest solution was to take over the part of the Market House shown above; the building, shown below, was erected in 1894 and used not only as a library but also as Municipal Buildings, Science and Art School, which facts are inscribed above the first-floor windows but few passers-by notice it.

THE STORY OF FALMOUTH'S SUCCESSIVE FIRE BRIGADES deserves a book of its own and there are several interesting episodes related in other pages of this one. In the space available here I shall concentrate on this brigade photograph taken sometime in the early 1920s outside the fire station, built in 1895, with one of its foundation stones, laid by the mayor, Mr H. Liddicoat, visible on the wall behind. Standing on and around their new steam fire-engine, which was only broken up in the late 1940s, are the members of the brigade, from left to right: Capt. H. Kelway; engineer W.H. Lawrence; firemen J. Brimacombe and P. Franklin; Sub-Capt. H.E. Tresidder; firemen J. Smith, C. Rowe and A. McCartney; and bugler A. Fray (in front). The whiskered gentleman to the right looked after the horses. For those about to ask, 'Why a bugler?' the answer was, how else could the brigade be easily assembled in pre-telephone days?

THE TOWN HALL was purpose-built on the Moor in 1864 to replace the one in the High Street, but was soon taken over by the Magistrates' Court and the functions of local government moved to the nearby Passmore Edwards building in 1894 (p. 69). To the left, the fire station, erected in 1895, shows the unusual aperture constructed to admit the wheeled ladder used by the brigade. The chimney belonged to Carne's Brewery.

THIS MID-1930S PHOTOGRAPH shows the Odeon cinema under construction on the site of the former Carne's Brewery. This most attractive cinema was, in turn, demolished to make way for a large supermarket with far less visual appeal than either of its predecessors. The small shop on the left bears an old Borough coat of arms acknowledging the fact that it had been built as one of the town's earliest public conveniences!

FALMOUTH WAS GRANTED A MARKET in 1652 during the Commonwealth, and the new Market House was built in 1812/13 on the Moor. By the end of the century it was not large enough to house all the stalls on market days and the open space in the lower Moor became the Market Place. It is marked as such on an Ordnance Survey map of 1880. The date of the top picture is uncertain but it is probably from 1894/5 and shows the entrance to the Market House to the right of the stalls; the bottom picture dates from 1894 when the Passmore Edwards Library was under construction and shows Carne's brewery chimney.

SECTION FOUR

The Sea Front

FALMOUTH'S SEA FRONT in the 1880s presents a truly rural picture. The trees in the middle distance show the location of the Gyllyngdune Estate, established in the 1830s by the Revd W.J. Coope (pp. 56/7), but at this time under the ownership of Sampson Waters, a local businessman. The Falmouth Hotel, shown prior to its 1898 addition, opened in 1865 and was built near the new railway terminus by a consortium of local businessmen to tempt up-country people to travel to Falmouth in comfort and take advantage of the mild climate and coastal scenery. This, without doubt, marked the beginning of Falmouth's tourist industry.

37031 FF&Cº

THIS 1895 PHOTOGRAPH shows the inevitable development further west along the sea front as more visitors discovered Falmouth which was being advertised as a health resort, and more accommodation became necessary for those wishing to take advantage of the sea air, scenery and bathing facilities. From 1865 the beach in front of the Falmouth Hotel remained private with a small landing jetty for pleasure boats. No doubt as a result of growing demand, the Falmouth Hotel Company built a second hotel, the Pendennis, in 1893, seen here on the extreme left. Next to the Falmouth is a building which originally consisted of five separate dwellings – two lodging houses, two private houses and the headquarters of the Coastguard Paymaster. This has become the Madeira Hotel. The building under construction next to that was to become four separate boarding houses until combined as the Gwendra Hotel in the 1920s. A few years later Cliffe House and Carthion were built west of the Pendennis and occupied by Mr de Pass, wealthy businessman and philanthropist, and by Mr J.A. Freeman the well-known local granite merchant who had moved here from Woodlane House and whose granite works were alongside the Penryn River. In those days the only sea-front road ran in front of these houses; the Gyllyngdune Estate remained an obstacle and there was no road as yet in front of the Falmouth. To the right, the headquarters of the Coastguard in Falmouth consisted of offices, with the flagpole, stores, accommodation for the Chief Officer and fourteen 'cottages' for the boatmen and gunnery instructor. In the background the rapidly expanding town has stretched across the whole of the flat hilltop with large private houses occupying the wooded, south-facing slope.

GYLLYNGDUNE ROAD, FALMOUTH

IN 1903 the obstacle of the Gyllyngdune Estate was finally breached and these photographs show part of the newly constructed extension to the sea front road. The estate had been bought from Coope by businessman Sampson Waters in 1863, and he later sold it to Mr F.J. Horniman, the local MP, from whom the Borough Council bought it. In the lower picture the notice-board advertises the land as the 'Horniman Estate'. Part was sold off by the Council for house and hotel development; the rest became the Winter Gardens, later changed to Gyllyngdune Gardens. When he had lived there, Revd Coope had built what has since been mistakenly called the Gyllyngdune Chapel, but this was never consecrated and was almost certainly a summer-house on the cliff top. Nearby a set of spiral steps led to a tunnel from which steps led down to Coope's private beach; both are seen above. In 1859/60 Coope was in controversy with the Waywardens over a footpath somewhere on the estate and it is likely that the path in question was the one shown in the lower picture, running along the cliff top on the seaward side of the road; its extent still coincides with the exact limits of his former estate.

Gyllyngdune Road (II), Falmouth.

BY 1907 THE SEA-FRONT ROAD extended from the Falmouth Hotel to Gyllyngvase Beach. Only the section in front of the Falmouth remained to connect Cliff Road, as it was now being called, with the Castle Drive. This section was traversed by a narrow promenade, known as Invalids' Walk (above), perpetuating Falmouth's image as a health resort. In 1908 the Corporation bought this strip of land from the Falmouth Hotel Company with the persuasive help of Mr John Barker MP, 'whose enthusiasm, energy and tact at length overcame the objections of the War Office to selling the requisite land', as the *Cornish Echo* newspaper reported. On 31 July 1908, in the presence of a large crowd, the road (below), decorated with flags and floral arches, was officially opened by the Rt Hon. R.B. Haldane, His Majesty's Secretary of State for War, using a key to unlock a barrier.

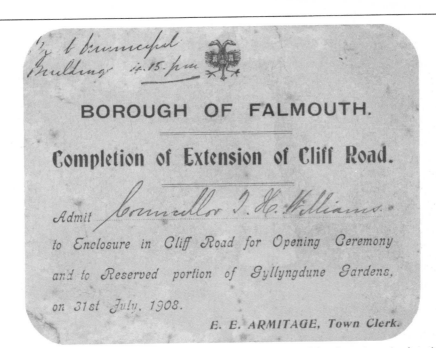

[handwritten notes at top: "To the Municipal Buildings 4.15 p.m."]

BOROUGH OF FALMOUTH.

Completion of Extension of Cliff Road.

Admit *Councillor J. H. Williams.*

to Enclosure in Cliff Road for Opening Ceremony

and to Reserved portion of Gyllyngdune Gardens,

on 31st July, 1908.

E. E. ARMITAGE, Town Clerk.

APPARENTLY, THE OBJECTIONS TO THE PURCHASE OF THE LAND had been based on the fact that Pendennis Point was a military base, bristling with coastal artillery, and in his speech in Gyllyngdune Gardens following the opening (above), Mr Haldane spoke not so much about the road extension he had just opened but used the occasion as a recruiting speech for the newly established Territorial Forces which had recently replaced the Militia. In these pictures, especially the one below of the newly opened extension, other notable features are: the row of Coastguard cottages overlooking the bay; at a higher level, army accommodation built in 1901/2 to house the permanent staff of the castle garrison; and, on the flat top of the headland, the prominent water tower used when army training necessitated a tented camp on the Hornworks.

THE DATES ON THIS PHOTOGRAPH are somewhat misleading. They refer to HMS *St Vincent* which was broken up in Falmouth docks in 1906 (see p. 88). One of its anchors was displayed in a chained enclosure behind Gyllyngvase Beach. It was taken away to be used as scrap during the Second World War. Falmouth was the destination for several of the old 'wooden walls' once the Navy had accepted iron ships. Some, like the St Vincent, were broken up, usually by Harris Brothers; others were used as various categories of training ship for boys.

FALMOUTH SWIMMING CLUB, founded in 1886, was based on Gyllyngvase Beach, first in a small changing hut but, as the club's membership grew, especially during the First World War when ladies were admitted, the larger premises, shown above, were built. The highlight of the year was the opening dip, usually in May, at 7.30 a.m., after which members were invited to 'St Michaels', then a private house, for breakfast. Swimming galas were held off the beach, and remembered even to this day is the occasion when the Mayor and other local dignitaries were coming ashore from the rafts when a large wave tipped them all into the shallow water, much to the collective amusement of the spectators.

IN THIS PICTURE, dating from about the turn of the century, before the Gyllyngdune Estate was bought by the Council, the land behind the beach had not been built over. One road, from Melvill Road, has been laid but the present Gyllyngvase Hill is only a path. Some houses have been built on Gyllyngvase Terrace. In the later years of the nineteenth century this had become the main bathing beach because it was the most easily accessible part of the sea front from the expanding town. The Swimming Club building is shown at the back of the beach below the road junction and there are a few people bathing at low tide but, apart from a few changing tents, there are none of the facilities associated with a beach today. The wheeled structure above high-water mark in the centre of the beach suggests that pleasure boats plied from here and this device enabled passengers to get on and off the boat without getting their feet wet. On the near side of the wooded Gyllyngdune Estate there is no sign of the Bay Hotel, built by the Falmouth Hotel Company in 1909 on a grassy bank well above road level.

HENRI SALMET first visited Falmouth in June 1912 when he landed his 50 hp Bleriot plane in fields near Union Corner. To advertise the *Daily Mail*, he flew over the town and harbour the next day, to be greeted by ships' sirens and general excitement for aeroplanes were a novelty in those days. His second visit, also sponsored by the *Daily Mail*, was in April 1914 when he landed on Gyllyngvase Beach but the wheels sank into the sand and the plane tipped up on its nose (above); Salmet, strapped in, was unhurt. The bent propellor was changed overnight by his crew and the aircraft pulled to the water's edge where the wheels were replaced by floats (below). Next day he took the mayoress, Mrs Chard, and, later, the mayor for a flight over the district. The following day he took off to fly to Penzance, again accompanied by the mayoress, but engine trouble over the bay forced him to land near the Manacles; this unusual incident was dealt with by the Coastguard who contacted Falmouth and the tug *Marion* came out with the mayor on board. The plane was towed all the way to Penzance with the mayoress still aboard, despite the choppy weather.

AT 2 A.M. ON CHRISTMAS MORNING 1935, the 160 ton French schooner *Loustic* of Libourne, bound from Quimper in Brittany to Cardiff to pick up a cargo of coal, ran ashore on rocks east of Gyllyngvase Beach. Her crew of five got ashore safely by lowering a ladder at low tide and walking up the beach, whence they were taken to the Royal Cornwall Sailors' Home. Later, they collected their belongings from the ship but their dog had to be destroyed. Within days, heavy seas had reduced the vessel to a pile of broken wood.

AMONG THE MANY SUGGESTIONS made around the turn of the century, meant to improve the health of the people of Falmouth, it was recommended that there should be more recreational areas and parks. Behind Gyllyngvase Beach stood an area of malodorous marsh which became the subject of complaint as housing spread to this part of the town. The land was given by Lord Kimberley, reclamation was paid for by Mrs Goldman, wife of the local MP, and it was converted into an attractive garden of lawns and flowerbeds with the original stream flowing through. Opened in 1910, it was called Queen Mary Gardens. The roof of the first Swimming Club hut is visible over the heads of the parading gentry.

SWANPOOL BEACH, in geological terms, is a storm beach, having been built up by large waves throwing sand and shingle above high tide level, thus blocking the entrance of a narrow tidal inlet and creating a lake, Swanpool. At one time the road into Falmouth ran across the beach, climbed Hangman's Hill and entered the town along Pennance Road and Woodlane; no road ran alongside the pool. It flooded frequently as its only drainage outlet was by means of seepage through the beach, but in 1826 a tunnel was dug 240 ft long and 4 ft high by a man and a boy. A road could now run behind the beach and alongside the pool with less danger of its overflowing.

This part of Cornwall is not rich in mineral deposits but there are veins of lead ore, galena, which sometimes contain worthwhile quantities of silver. The ore was discovered behind Swanpool Beach, below Tremorvah Farm, and although it had been worked spasmodically before this date, its heyday began in 1851 when a local newspaper reported 'Swanpool Mine ... idle for a long series of years ... is retaken up by a number of wealthy adventurers,' meaning people who were prepared to invest money in it. Between 1851 and 1856 three shafts were sunk, the deepest to eighty fathoms, and a 40 in steam-engine installed. The ore was rich near the surface but became poorer deeper down with the addition of troublesome arsenic which had to be removed before the ore was smelted. In the fields south of the beach shown opposite the company built what was then the most efficient plant in Cornwall to remove the impurity, and to disperse the dangerous fumes a brick-lined tunnel was dug to a chimney at the end of the point. Later the tunnel was extended to a second chimney on

the highest point of the headland to improve the draught. These features are clearly seen in the picture above. The chimneys were named Anna-Maria and Caroline for the Fox family were among the adventurers, and the headland is called 'the Stack' to this day on account of the chimneys. Anna-Maria was blown down in a gale and Caroline demolished around 1890. Over 100 people were employed in the mine, including twenty 'bal maidens', girls employed on the surface sorting the ore. Water pumped out of the mine was led to the sea along wooden launders but by 1860 the deeper levels had become expensive to pump – locally the mine was referred to as 'Wheal Swamp-All' – and the operation was abandoned. During the Second World War American engineers spread the waste tip (opposite) over the marshy land behind the beach and fire-fighting exercises were conducted there. Since then the area has become a car park, the buildings beside the chimney demolished and those on the left replaced by holiday flats; only the lower part of the chimney remains as evidence of the only real mining operation in Falmouth. The picture above illustrates the difficulty of transport in Cornwall at that time. Carriage of heavy or bulky goods by land was both slow and costly, and where practicable they were taken as near their destination as possible by water. Here a trading ketch has been driven up on the beach and timber, probably for the mine, is being unloaded.

THE REMAINS OF THE OLD ARSENIC WORKS are seen here with the more recent addition, in the centre, of the studio of well-known local artist, Henry Scott Tuke, who lived in the nearby house. He painted mainly local scenes, ships and people, many of them in the small cove on the extreme left, known today as Tuke's Cove. The road coming down the hill ran straight across behind the beach until a storm destroyed it in 1917; its foundations may sometimes be seen after a storm, buried in the beach. The new road with the S-bend we see today was built further inland, but this too is often buried under sand and shingle when storm waves have swept across the beach on to the car park.

THE CHIMNEY CALLED CAROLINE commands a fine view of the entrance to Falmouth harbour from its position on Pennance Point. Parts of the brick-lined tunnel leading to it may still be seen beside the footpath round the headland.

The Docks and the Railway

FALMOUTH DOCKS had its origin among those businessmen of the town who realized that if the port were to keep the Packet Service facilities for the new steam-driven ships would have to be improved. Although they failed in this aim, the Falmouth Docks Company was formed after a public meeting at the Town Hall on 31 May 1858, and the Docks was planned on an area of about 150 acres on the sheltered north side of the Pendennis headland. A natural feature known as Bar Point projected northwards at this point, towards Trefusis Point, and offered a good foundation for a breakwater. Around it, especially on the town side where a large floating dock – today we should call it a 'tidal basin' – was planned, the water was shallow and needed extensive deepening. This ancient vessel, *Briton*, was responsible for much of the early dredging work to make access to the new docks and wharves possible. By 1860 a channel of deep water 300 ft wide had been dredged to connect the docks with the deep water in Carrick Roads to the east.

THERE WERE SEVERAL VERSIONS of the original plans for Falmouth Docks, drawn up by James Abernethy, but all that was constructed in the first instance can be seen in the picture above. The foundation stone of the new enterprise was laid with the usual Victorian pageantry by Lord Falmouth on 28 February 1860 – no trace of it can be found today – but the company was soon in financial trouble and shareholders authorized the directors to borrow £50,000 from the Public Loan Commissioners at $3\frac{1}{4}$% interest. By 1862 No. 1 Graving Dock had been completed, together with the large stone building, known as the grain store, seen on the extreme left. A year later the Eastern Breakwater (left) was opened and No. 2 Dock completed. Next year, 1864, the first cargo of china clay was loaded, brought along the newly-opened Cornwall Railway which had lines laid into the Docks, and the two breakwaters were extended almost to their full length. The directors had to borrow a further £20,000. At this stage in development the Western Breakwater had a bridge in it, probably at the point where the entrance to the floating dock was to be located, on the extreme right of the picture. But in 1865 the piles burst outwards and the Western Breakwater disappeared. Worse was yet to come. When the Bank of England raised the interest rate to 10 per cent on 11 May 1866, or Black Friday, all work in the Docks was suspended. Further disasters overtook the organization in the next few months. In January 1867 a very high tide and what the newspapers called a 'hurricane' badly damaged the Eastern Breakwater and two months later the brig *Uhla*, deserted by her crew, ran along the face of the same breakwater and displaced many piles. In October of that same year shareholders authorized the directors to hand over possession of the works to the Public Works Loan Commissioners, and in December their Secretary and Solicitors came to Falmouth to take possession. By 1869 the Eastern Breakwater had been repaired at a cost of £8,500 and the docks entered a more trouble-free period. The proposed floating dock was ultimately abandoned, for which we should be eternally grateful.

INSIDE THE DOCKS IN THE EARLY DAYS it was possible for any organization to set up in business. Ship repairing, for example, was operated by an independent firm known first as the Docks, Foundry and Engineering Company but changed three years later, in 1871, to Cox and Co, which hired the dry docks from the Dock Company to carry out repairs. Other operations included fishing and the picture shows the Lowestoft fleet landing its catch on the beach now occupied by Nos 3 and 4 docks. The proximity of the railway station meant that fish landed here could be taken to the loading platform by the horse-drawn carts and then to up-country markets by rail. So many different organizations operated on Dock Company land before the First World War that the area was more industrial estate than dockyard. It was run for many years by two well-respected men, F.J. Bowles, general manager and J.B. Tilly, engineer. Companies included Pool, Skinner and Williams, shipbuilders; J.M. Goodman, miller (steam), general merchant, haulage contractor, steam-roller and thrashing [*sic*] machine proprietor; S. and T. Trounson, grain merchant (much of south Cornwall's grain and flour was distributed from here); G.C. Fox and Co., timber merchants; Harvey and Co., timber merchant; Walter Sandover, salvage contractor; Cornish Coal Cooperative Ltd (the vessel alongside the northern breakwater in the picture opposite is a coal hulk from which ships were refuelled); Harris Bros, shipbreakers; Hurrell and Co., grain merchants; H. Leetham and Sons, flour merchants; Samuel Warwick, oilcake merchant; Gordon Murdoch, ship broker; Angelo Parodi, fish merchant; Powell and Hough, shipowners; Joseph Rank Ltd, corn merchant; Rickard and Moseley, coal merchants; and the St Keverne Stone Company. The Eastern Breakwater was the passenger terminal for vessels of the British and Irish Steam Packet Company which ran regularly from London to Dublin, calling at Portsmouth, Southampton, Plymouth and Falmouth. They operated 'six large and powerful steamers', accordingly to their advertisements, 'twice weekly, carrying cargo, passengers and livestock' and up to 1914 many people with time to do so chose to travel the whole or part of the way to and from London by boat.

MANY DIFFERENT TYPES OF VESSEL used the dry docks. Above, the old 'wooden wall', HMS *St Vincent*, is in No. 2 dock being broken up, probably by Harris Bros. After the Navy had turned to steam-driven steel ships, redundant vessels such as this were used for a variety of purposes, including training boys for naval service (pp. 124–5) and target practice, although some proved very difficult to sink. The anchor already seen at Gyllyngvase (p. 78) may be the one seen here to the left of the dock head although such a ship would carry more than one anchor. Below, in 1905, more modern steamers occupy both docks, which in this instance are truly 'dry', the water having been pumped out by the machinery housed beside the chimney at the dock gate. The vessel in No. 1 dock is *Lady of the Isles*, a former Isles of Scilly ferry. The large shed shown on both photographs to the left of No. 2 dock entrance is the RNLI boathouse, in which the port's lifeboat was kept until docks reorganization after 1918 forced the lifeboat to be anchored afloat.

OF THE MANY WRECKED, DERELICT, STORM-DAMAGED OR BROKEN-DOWN VESSELS to arrive in Falmouth for repair, the stern half of the *Highland Fling* was one of the most unusual. Bound from London to Buenos Aires in January 1907, with a cargo of 3,000 tons of cement, the 2,679 ton vessel sprang a leak in the Channel and came in to Falmouth for examination by a diver. After patching-up, her owners decided to send her to Cardiff to discharge cargo and undergo repair. She left in fair weather, encountered fog towards the Lizard and went aground two hours later at Enys Point, near Cadgwith. The Falmouth tugs *Triton*, *Victor*, and *Eagle* tried to pull her off at high tide a few hours later but the bow section was firmly wedged and all efforts failed. The crew were taken off and accommodated in the Falmouth Sailors' Home but the officers stayed on board. Part of the cargo was unloaded into lighters. Further attempts to pull the vessel free were to no avail and Capt. Anderson of the West of England Salvage Company decided that the stern section, containing the engines and valuable refrigeration machinery should be separated from the bow by explosives. This was gradually done until only the keel remained to be separated when a strong easterly gale blew up and the waves completed the job of separation, the keel breaking with the rolling of the ship. The Falmouth tugs put lines aboard immediately and towed the vessel back to the harbour she had left only two weeks previously. After having been grounded in the shallows near the Governor buoy and her cargo and bunker coal removed, the stern was taken slowly into the docks. Meanwhile, the bow section had been completely broken up in strong winds and heavy seas, a fate which the stern must have shared had the separation not taken place. Plans to build a new bow section to this part, seen here in No. 2 dock, were not pursued and in late April the vessel was undocked and moved alongside the Eastern Breakwater ready to be broken up by Harris Bros. The captain had his certificate suspended for six months after a hearing in Liverpool, the grounding being attributed to his lack of care in navigating the vessel.

THE OLDEST BUILDING IN TODAY'S DOCKS is known as the Grain Store; built of local stone, it is now a listed building and, as one of the few parts of the original docks to survive, should be preserved for all time.

THE GLASGOW STEAMER *STRATHLYON* developed a leak off the Lizard in January 1908, and made for Falmouth. Once in No. 2 dock, a large explosion blew off the hatches and started a serious fire in the cargo of 'fusil oil', potato meal, palm oil, sugar and toys'. Coastguards, soldiers from the castle, sailors from HMS *Julia*, anchored in the harbour, and the town firefighters together brought the blaze under control but the ship was seriously damaged.

DURING THE FIRST WORLD WAR control of the docks was taken over by the Admiralty and the building of No. 3 dock commenced, larger than those already built. By 1917, as a result of the German submarine offensive, ship repair had assumed enormous strategic importance but the workforce and facilities in Falmouth were totally inadequate to deal with the added workload of damaged vessels. A London firm of ship repairers, R. H. Green and Silley Weir, was asked to investigate the situation and after sending workmen down to help clear the repair congestion, its managing director realized the potential of Falmouth and eventually, in 1918, bought the dockyard. Under the new name of Silley Cox and Co., great improvements were undertaken; more skilled workmen were brought from London, new workshops built and new machinery installed. Soon after this aerial photograph was taken, showing the *Empress of Scotland* in the recently completed No. 3 dock, in 1924 a fourth dry dock was built and opened in 1928. Eventually, new wharves were constructed on the western side of the Western Breakwater (see p. 92) and the full potential of Falmouth as one of the world's major ship repair ports was at last realized. Apart from the docks, several other interesting features are shown on this photograph. At the top right the Bar area is seen at high tide, surrounded as it was by small shipyards; in the centre, the close relationship between the railway station and the docks, with the connecting railway line, is illustrated. On Pendennis headland, the Castle Drive overlooks the docks, making it a popular viewpoint, and the row of Coastguard cottages stands in an isolated, curving row; today they are engulfed by recent housing development.

THE BOOM IN SHIP REPAIR after the Second World War is illustrated above with sixteen vessels, mostly tankers, alongside. The wharves built between the wars are shown: from the nearest, Queen's (1938–42), Empire (1931–3) and King's (1935–7). Below, the same scene taken about five years later from a different viewpoint shows the most recent wharves, Duchy and County, built during the prosperous 1950s on the town side of the dockyard. At this time, the repair workload necessitated the employment of two floating docks, shown clearly on both pictures. Attempts to make Falmouth the principal world port for tanker repair and tank cleaning were thwarted by foreign competition and the increase in the size of tankers, despite the enlargement of No. 2 dock, opened and named the Queen Elizabeth Dock by HRH the Duke of Edinburgh in 1958.

ANOTHER SIGNIFICANT DEVELOPMENT of the 1860s was the arrival of the railway in the town, and an early locomotive, *Mazeppa*, is shown here with three carriages at the road bridge near the station. In 1846 the West Cornwall Railway had joined Penzance with Truro (Newham Quay), and Falmouth eventually became the terminus of the Cornwall Railway from Plymouth. This line had reached Truro in 1859, the year the Royal Albert Bridge across the Tamar was opened, but it was four years before the section to Falmouth was completed. Original plans were for the terminus to be located at Greenbank but once the docks were established, it was moved further south to the location shown on p. 91. At first the Cornwall Railway, in common with the whole of what became the Great Western Railway in 1889, was built on the broad gauge of 7 ft 0¼ in, while the West Cornwall Railway was on the narrower standard gauge of 4 ft 8½ in. The obvious problem of this difference was overcome, in Cornwall at least, by laying a third rail along the West Cornwall line, a technique known as 'mixed gauge'. Eventually, however, to conform with the rest of the country, the GWR between Exeter and Falmouth was converted to standard gauge in two days – 20 and 21 May 1892 – in a massive operation, the organization of which required a handbook of fifty-five pages.

ONE OF THE REASONS for the late arrival of the railway in Falmouth was the large number of deep valleys which needed viaducts; originally there were eight between Truro and Falmouth, all of them with wooden superstructure and known as 'fan' viaducts, such as that over the Carnon Valley, above. Maintenance problems and costs led to these being changed between 1923 and 1934, five of them being converted to embankments and three, Carnon, Ponsanooth and College, Penryn, to viaducts with block or concrete piers and arches. The lower picture shows the College viaducts, old and new, alongside each other before the timber superstructure was removed to leave the old pillars which, in all three valleys, are still in position today.

ON MONDAY 31 OCTOBER 1898, the 5.20 train from Falmouth, consisting of engine No. 3542, two carriages and a mail van, was derailed about 250 yd on the Falmouth side of Hillhead bridge. The engine and mail van ran down the 70 ft embankment and turned over. The fireman jumped off with a badly scalded arm and four passengers were injured, but driver Cotterill stayed on the footplate, was badly scalded and later died. Sixty yards of track were torn up and in the picture above a rescue train has arrived on the scene to begin recovery operations.

ANOTHER ACCIDENT ON THE BRANCH LINE occurred during the Second World War in the cutting between the Pennance Road bridge and Swanvale when, on 11 January 1941, as the Germans were bombing the town, carriages were derailed as bombs fell nearby, leaving a large crater in an allotment garden and fracturing a petrol pipeline.

FALMOUTH RAILWAY STATION was once described as a 'noble erection', as befitted the terminus of the Cornwall Railway. The passenger shed was completely roofed with the largest span in Cornwall at that time; its refreshment room was said to be too small for so important a station so a new one was built. There was a separate engine house and turntable, goods shed and fish platform. In the picture above, a horse bus leaves the station approach road, no doubt with passengers for one of the town's large hotels, each of which had its own bus, while, below, the first ever motor bus or passenger-car leaves the station for an Easter Monday excursion in 1904. Imagine the discomfort with those solid tyres. Other stations in Falmouth came later: Penmere Halt in 1925 was for dock workers from Swanvale, which had been built to house them; the Dell (now Falmouth Town) the result of complaints that the former 'main' station, now degraded by almost total demolition to one platform and called Falmouth Docks, was too far from the town's residential and shopping area.

The Waterfront

THE TIDE MILL ON THE BAR ceased to operate in 1862 and this photograph taken three decades later shows that its main working features remained. The sluices on both sides of the mill lead into the mill pool shown here full of water as it was being used as a timber pool for seasoning wood used in nearby boatyards. The horse is hauling baulks of timber from the pool to the sawpit of one of the yards. Other features of interest are the Killigrew Monument in the background, and, on the skyline, the town's first Observatory, built by the Royal Cornwall Polytechnic Society in 1867 when it embraced meteorology as a developing science and maintained the connection with weather records until the early 1950s.

ONE OF THE SEVERAL BOATYARDS around the Bar was that of W.E. Thomas, three generations of which family carried on building wooden boats here up to 1926. The photograph of workers and apprentices seen above with Mr W.E. Thomas, third from the left, was taken around 1905 and also shows the Submarine Pier, the low tide reflection of which makes it look higher than it was. The sheds behind the group on the end of the Bar itself, were in the yard of Symonds Brothers, the left one being a tidal shed so that boats could be brought under cover and worked on. Off picture to the left was one of the town's sewage tanks, part of the earliest sewerage system into which effluent was piped. When full it was emptied into a hopper barge and taken out to sea for dumping. Mr Bert Thomas, the third generation to run the yard and my informant on this aspect of Falmouth's waterfront, emphasized that when the tank was being emptied it was advisable to find a job elsewhere for a few hours.

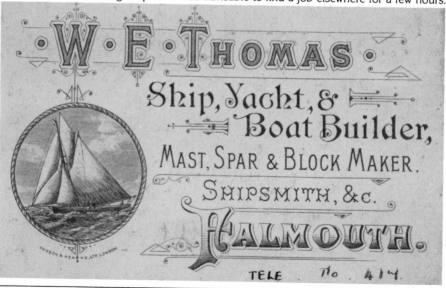

FALMOUTH BECAME A LIFEBOAT STATION in 1867 when the *City of Gloucester*, presented by the people of that city, was given free carriage to Falmouth by the GWR and a large crowd saw the vessel paraded through the town, drawn by twelve horses, before she was launched and her self-righting qualities tested. Her only work in twenty years was to stand by a vessel in difficulties and in 1887, she was replaced by the *Jane Whittingham*, a ten-oared boat whose seven years in the port were uneventful. This picture probably shows the *Jane Whittingham* with cox'n, Sam Hingston, standing on the extreme left at the tiller.

THE SHED IN THE DOCKS had to be enlarged in 1894 when a longer, twelve-oared boat, which was to become famous in the port, arrived. The *Bob Newbon*, is seen on exercise in this picture. She took an active part in many rescues, notably those of *Mohegan* in 1898 and *Paris* in 1899, both on the Manacles. In her twenty-five years in Falmouth she saved fifty-eight lives.

BOB NEWBON LIES ALONGSIDE TOWN QUAY soon after one of her most dramatic rescues with her crew of fifteen aboard. They were, right to left: Willie Tonkin, Arthur Jones, Johnny James, Willie Leuty (bowman), Fred Cabot, 'Happy' Jack Smith, Bobby Toms, Jack Rolling; then four men, front to back, Reggie Tonkin, Edwin Jones, ? Tuffery, George Jones; then Tom Pollard, Sam Hingston, (cox'n). The identity of the man on the extreme left is not known. On 1 February 1914 the German four-masted barque *Hera*, from Chile, 1,994 tons, with a cargo of nitrate and twenty-four crew, was approaching Falmouth 'for orders'. Past the Lizard the vessel lost her bearings, and in the dark missed St Anthony light and passed the harbour entrance. In squally weather *Hera* ran heavily on to a reef surrounding Gull Rock in Gerrans Bay and sank in ten minutes at about 11.30 p.m. All the crew got into one lifeboat which was soon capsized by heavy seas and only nine managed to scramble back on to the sinking vessel, clambering up the mast as she settled on the bottom. One of the crew possessed a whistle which, blown continuously, attracted villagers' attention, but they were powerless to help as the tide rose higher up the mast. Portloe Coastguard sent a message to Falmouth Lifeboat which left moorings soon after midnight, towed by the tug *Perran*, but in the heavy seas did not reach *Hera* until 3.30 a.m. By then three of the men on the mast had slipped off, exhausted, and the mate died lashed to the rigging. The lifeboat found difficulty in locating them until she heard the whistle above the wind and sea and picked up the five survivors from what was left of the mast above the water, five hours after their ordeal had begun. Sam Hingston, cox'n, said later, 'On the way we encountered huge seas. When about a mile off the shore we slipped the *Perran* and went in between the Gull Rock and Nare Head and spoke to the coastguards, who were out on the rocks. From what we could ascertain from them there was a vessel near the shore, but on the outside of us. All at once, I heard a whistle blowing. We immediately got our anchor up and went away in the direction of the sound. Then we saw something like a speck on our bow and later we made out five men hanging on to a spar. We experienced considerable difficulty in rescuing the men owing to heavy seas; we were afraid of crushing them against the spar. Our bowman, Willie Leuty, had his finger badly crushed. One of the men was in a state of collapse and we were afraid he would not survive.' As the bodies were recovered, they were buried in Veryan churchyard in a solemn and impressive service at which Chaplain J.C. Badger of the Falmouth Seamen's Bethel assisted.

THESE TWO VIEWS OF THE BAR from opposite viewpoints show the overwhelming importance of shipbuilding in that area. Taken from the unusual vantage point of the old Observatory tower, the scene above shows several ships under construction or repair, both steel ships in the tidal water to the left and wooden vessels on the slipways on the extreme right. Although taken about thirty years later, the lower view shows the Observatory tower on the skyline and the shipyards in the foreground, dominated by the sheds of Cox and Co. The railway goods shed, to the right of the station in the first view, stands in the foreground in the second, while the Submarine Pier which protrudes beyond the sheds does not appear in the older picture.

THIS CLOSE-UP, SEA LEVEL PHOTOGRAPH of the tidal Bar Creek shows boats and hulks afloat soon after the First World War. The chimney left of the centre, part of the engine which drove a steam saw, stood in the boatyard of W.H. Lean who lived in Armyn Villa on the extreme left, later the headquarters of the Missions to Seamen. In Warn's 1864 Directory, some sixty years before the photograph was taken, the yard was described as: 'Ship and Boat Builder, Ship Smith etc., Bar and Greenbank, Falmouth. Masts and spars of every description. New and second-hand boats always on sale. All kinds of ship work done by contract'. To the right of the chimney is the tower which gave its name to Tower House, supposedly erected by an old sea captain who wished to have a view of both harbour and bay, visible from here before the houses in Melvill Road were built. Later it became the Officers' Mess for the castle garrison for a time. The houses built well above road level in Bar Road stand out clearly, while the buildings below them, on the seaward side of the road, were themselves well above shipyard level and their lower storeys were used by the yards for storage. At one time there was a limekiln on the extreme right of the photograph and the house there was called Limekiln Cottage until its demolition.

BANK PLACE AND GROVE PLACE are seen here in the early part of the century when the sea came up to the road. The pier to left of the Killigrew Monument was known as the Submarine Pier up to its demolition in the mid-1980s, although it had nothing to do with submarines. As part of the country's sea defences in the latter part of the last century, harbours such as Falmouth were protected by electrically detonated mines laid on the sea floor and controlled by a branch of the Militia known as the 'Submarine Miners, Royal Engineers'. This unit operated from the barracks beyond the Monument and a narrow gauge railway line connected them with the pier (built 1892) and its crane to facilitate loading the equipment on to a boat. After 1904 other methods of defence rendered this type of mine obsolete but the pier remained and was used for a variety of purposes up to the Second World War after which it was neglected and deterioration led to its demolition in 1985. Much of the material excavated from the docks was dumped here in the 1930s and the reclaimed land has fulfilled many purposes since then. During the preparations for D-Day, the US Navy took it over for maintenance of its landing craft and after the war it became the headquarters of the RAF Air-Sea Rescue Service, then a dinghy 'hard' and car park. Changes since then have reclaimed even more land from the sea as part of the Port Pendennis development.

PART OF THE PENZANCE FISHING FLEET is seen here in the basin at Town Quay around the turn of the century and certainly before 1903 when the arm on the right, behind the ships' masts, was widened at the same time as the Prince of Wales Pier was lengthened. These pilchard 'drivers' were in Falmouth because the shoals they were following and catching were nearer to Falmouth than their home port and they had come in to land their catches, probably in the docks which, up to the First World War, was the harbour's fishing base (p. 87). It is likely that this picture of inactivity was taken on a Sunday as no fishing was ever done on the Sabbath by Cornish boats – and the two children seem to be dressed in their Sunday best. One of the boats in the centre of the picture is named after Agnes Weston (1840–1918), better known to sailors as Aggie Weston. This remarkable lady was a tireless welfare worker on behalf of seamen and founded 'Royal Sailors' Rests' at Devonport, Portsmouth and Chatham, as well as rest homes in many other ports all of which were open to seamen in need of rest and accommodation. She encouraged Christian tolerance and temperance. The large vessel whose stern can be seen in the background is a three-masted schooner probably unloading on North Quay.

ALTHOUGH NOW LARGELY A TOURIST FACILITY, the complex of quays built by Peter Killigrew in 1670 were used for commercial purposes until the 1930s. In the picture above, the trading ketch, *Regina*, is unloading what appears to be stone for road-making, probably from the Lizard quarries. A vessel of this size could not get into the basin today because of silting. The buildings behind the quay are, from left to right: the Custom House, Harbourmaster's Officer, Globe Hotel, Tregye Café (formerly the Ship Inn), Larcombe, engraver, and the Marine Hotel. In former times there were many more inns in the quay area and the Electric Telegraph Office was located in this vicinity after 1857. The northern part of the quays was at one time the domain of the coal merchants and, below, coal is being unloaded from the well-known topsail schooner, *Mary Barrow*. Built in the Bar yard of W.H. Lean in 1891, the vessel had several owners, including Lean, who used her in the Newfoundland trade; others used her for coal carrying in the 1920s and, later, general coastal trade. She was lost off the Isle of Man in 1938.

190. Schooner Lizzie Ellen. After the gale. *epic Photo.*

SEVERAL BOATS OF VARYING SIZE shelter in the Town Quay basin, including the trading schooner *Lizzie Ellen*, its topsail in tatters while, on the outer side of the quay, a harbour tug takes on water. The tall building in the left background, with the fence surrounding its flat roof, is the British and Foreign Sailors' Society and Seamen's Institute, as the name board indicates. The lower building in front of it was for many years a workshop for a firm of marine engineers; now it is a restaurant. The space on the quay between the buildings was occupied by the lifeboat house after the post-First-World-War docks expansion had made it necessary for the lifeboat to move to a permanent mooring. The crew's equipment and clothing were kept in it in readiness for an emergency, but it was so small not all of them could change at the same time ... so, in the early 1980s a new, larger, much better equipped boathouse replaced it, built with money raised locally by a very active and persuasive committee.

THIS WAS ONCE A WORKING QUAY, called North Quay; now it is a residential and tourist area called King Charles' Quay. The sheds built here were used for storage by the local coal merchants.

THIS BROAD ARM on the south side of Town Quay basin has always been a favourite strolling and chatting place for townsfolk. There is always so much to see and talk about, even though the activities around the quays have changed drastically since this early twentieth-century photograph was taken. The low building in the centre was used for many years by local artist, Henry Scott Tuke, while behind it were workshops. The flag pole standing in front of what was then the Harbourmaster's Office was used to hoist a flag in rough weather to indicate that the local boatmen could charge double fare! In the left background are the Sailors' Home and Hospital (with the name board) and the Bank House Hotel.

TWO VIEWS OF QUAY HILL, with North Quay at the seaward end. The upper section (above) was mainly residential but only a few of the houses on the right have survived. The lower section (left) was lined mainly by taverns although, at the bottom right, the large lamp proclaims the location of the Seamen's Bethel, rebuilt in 1893.

THE FALMOUTH BRANCH of the British and Foreign Sailors' Society was established in 1849 for the use and welfare of sailors visiting the port. The Seamen's Bethel and Institute was the name given to it locally and in addition to the magnificent chapel, seen above, there were rest- and reading-rooms here, on the Quay, at Fish Strand (p. 110) and, during the First War, in the docks. One of the port's dedicated missionaries, Mr T.H.G. Roscorla, stands in this unique pulpit with, behind him, the two-manual organ given to the Bethel by Mrs R. Davey in memory of her husband. Beneath the pulpit, was the pump for the organ, usually worked by two lads, access to which was by a door in the 'port bow'. Services were held every Sunday at 6.30 and during the week as required. To enable the missionaries and other helpers to visit ships anchored in the harbour the Institute had three boats – *Clareen*, for Carrick Roads, and *Gift* and *Three Sisters* for the inner harbour. A notable annual event held in these spectacular surroundings was the harvest festival – the 'harvest of the sea' – which attracted big congregations. Many well-beloved Cornish seamen's hymns were lustily sung and the Bethel was decorated with nets, crabpots and other fishing equipment.

ON THE POSTCARD, dated 25 January 1906, from which this picture was taken, the writer describes this as 'the new room given to the Seamen's Bethel ... with Mr Badger, the chaplain, known among sailors all over the world as "the sailors' friend"...' The *Tocopilla Room*, as it became known, was given to the Bethel by Mr W.H. Williams who, in 1866, was a cashier at the local bank of J. Michael Williams and Co. By 1877 he had risen to be manager but his contacts with shipping from South America with cargoes of guano, for fertilizer, persuaded him to move a year later to Tocopilla in northern Chile where he went into business and eventually became British Consul. In 1899 he returned to Falmouth after his health had begun to fail and involved himself in town affairs. In 1905 he gave the Society £500 to build a new wing on the Bethel which was called the Tocopilla Room. A year later he gave £200 for the erection of the Fishermen's Rest at Fish Strand Quay (below) and just before he died in 1907, gave £50 for the Cabmen's Shelter and Fishermen's Rest at Prince of Wales Pier.

FALMOUTH BECAME THE FIRST CORNISH TOWN TO HAVE DOMESTIC GAS LIGHTING in 1819 when James Wynn, who had taken the lease of the Royal Hotel, had his own gas producing plant built in the yard behind the hotel. He sold surplus gas to neighbours and before long, realizing that there was money to be made in gas, let the hotel and built an enlarged gasworks on this waterfront site, which he owned, where it was easier to import coal. Not only did more and more shops buy his gas but by 1840 the streets were lit. There were many complaints over the inefficiency of the street lamps and Wynn had a protracted disagreement with the Vestry over the rating of his plant and pipes. After his death in 1849, at the age of 88, his son Robert took over the gasworks but there were still complaints about smell and discharge of tar into the harbour, as well as poor quality lighting. By 1860 the works had been sold to the Mead Brothers who, in turn, sold it to a consortium of local businessmen who formed the Falmouth Gas Light and Coke Company. Gas continued to be manufactured on this site into the 1950s when North Sea gas made it superfluous and it was cleared, extended and used as a car park. In the photograph the vessel alongside the gasworks is the schooner *Waterwitch*, one of the most famous of all British merchant ships. Built in 1872 at Poole, she was engaged in coastal trading until running aground outside Newlyn harbour. The wreck was bought and rebuilt by Edward Stephens of Fowey and *Waterwitch* spent the next eighteen years in the coasting trade, for much of the time carrying coal to Falmouth gasworks. She was one of the very few British vessels trading out of the UK in which steamship officers who wished to become pilots could obtain the square-rig qualification which, until 1937, was necessary to them. A stream of young men with masters' certificates signed on as mates but actually worked as crew. This made her one of the most celebrated of British merchantmen. She was laid up in 1936 and sold to Estonia in 1938. She had the distinction of being the last cargo-carrying British square-rigger in home waters.

FISH STRAND was so named because at this point, originally, was the beach or 'strand' where fish was landed for the fish market. A short pier was built early on and extended in 1871 at a cost of £808 17s. 6d. It was here that Chard's, one of the local fish merchants, built an iceworks which was demolished only when the large car park was built on the site of the former gasworks.

THE MARKET STRAND PIER was extended at the same time as Fish Strand and cost £1,867 17s. 6d. It became an excellent facility for the increasing number of pleasure boats using the harbour and here, taking advantage of the improvements, is the early Flushing steam ferry *Greyhound* waiting for passengers to board. There was, in fact, great congestion at times in the summer months and letters were written to local papers complaining of the 'unruly conduct' among captains.

THIS MORE COMPREHENSIVE VIEW of Market Strand Pier, with Fish Strand Quay further along on the right, shows how valuable it was for the large steam-driven pleasure boats such as *Queen of the Fal*. The story of these boats has been well presented in *Passenger Steamers of the River Fal* by Alan Kittridge, where the several competing shipping companies are described in detail. Two pleasure boats bore the name *Queen of the Fal* and both were built by Cox and Co. in Falmouth Docks. This is the first of that name, built in 1893 for Benney and Co. and used between Falmouth and Truro from April to October. In 1906 she was taken over by the River Fal Steamship Company but sold for towage purposes to the River Thames five years later. The Watermen's Rest is seen on the far side of the pier and to the right of the steps above the ship's bow, the plaque bears the simple inscription 'William Selley: Mayor: 1873'.

THIS TEMPORARY GRANDSTAND was erected on the Moor in July 1903, between the Mission church and Packet Memorial, to accommodate VIPs when the Prince of Wales (later King George V) with Princess (later Queen) Mary came to Falmouth for the ceremony of laying the foundation stone of Prince of Wales Pier. The royal couple are in the carriage being greeted by the mayor and watched by the guard of honour of Cornwall Rifle Volunteers and a group of freemasons. After this reception the whole party were to move to Market Strand Pier where large numbers of townsfolk and a carefully arranged group of girls from the Royal Cornwall Home awaited their arrival. Earlier that week, His Royal Highness had opened an extension to Truro Cathedral and had travelled down river from Tregothnan with Lord and Lady Falmouth, landing at the Submarine Pier.

TWO YEARS LATER, in May 1905, the completed pier extension was named and opened by the Earl of Kimberley whose father had laid the foundation stone of the earlier Market Strand Pier in 1871. The earl had accompanied his father on what had been his first visit to Falmouth. On this occasion the GWR had run excursion trains from all Cornish stations. Not only had the pier been lengthened but the old pier (the granite structure on the left) had been doubled in width. Plaques to commemorate all the foundation stone layings and openings are spaced along the pier today and a leisurely stroll along it not only gives a superb view of the inner harbour and waterfront but also supplies an interesting lesson in the local history of this notable part of the town. It was at this pier, in March 1942, that some of the survivors of Operation 'Chariot' landed on their return from St Nazaire. This successful but expensive raid on the docks destroyed the gate of the largest dry dock in western France, denying its use to the German Navy. Of 622 sailors and commandos that set out, 168 were killed and many taken prisoner; five Victoria Crosses were won. A plaque to remind us of this heroic action has been placed on the old gasworks car park by the St Nazaire Society.

HERE IS THE SITE of the original Mulberry Square, location of Falmouth's first Custom House and the homes of some of the town's earliest merchants. In this picture, 250 years later, it has become the coal-yard of Harris Brothers, and a collier unloads with the help of dockside cranes. On the skyline is the smoking chimney of the old electricity generating station. On the coal-yard site today is a modern housing complex known as Mulberry Court.

THE BEACH AT TURNPIKE CREEK, the graveyard of a number of formerly dignified and well-tended coastal schooners which where left to rot away, is now the site of Falmouth's biggest yacht marina. During the First World War owners were encouraged to keep these vessels in operation but, after 1918, many were laid up in creeks and estuaries all round the south-west when they were no longer profitable because steamers were taking over the coastal traffic and much of their trade had passed to the road and railway.

THE INNER HARBOUR with sailing craft at anchor, seen from Flushing, is made more interesting in this view by the unusual sight, on the left, of the engine house of Wheal Clinton. The same metal that was exploited at Swanpool was mined here and the ore was particularly rich in silver. But the galleries ran under the harbour and water forced the closure of the mine in 1858 after only five years of profitable working. The top part of the chimney was blown down in a severe gale a few years after the closure but the buildings seen in this photograph remained until replaced by houses.

A NUMBER OF ELDERLY WATERMEN operated their own ferry service between Greenbank and Flushing up to the late 1940s. The gentlemen pictured here are waiting for passengers off Flushing Quay and charged only 3d. for the pleasant and leisurely crossing.

IN THIS EARLY TWENTIETH-CENTURY VIEW of the Penryn River and the Greenbank area of Falmouth the steep slope rising from the water's edge and the terraces of houses built across it can be seen. Some of the terraces have still to be completed and the hill, known as the Beacon, in the background has still to be invaded by settlement. Along the waterfront, from right to left, stretch the Greenbank Hotel, workshops and coal-yard, Royal Cornwall Yacht Club and Well Beach, all running along in front of the row of opulent dwellings in Dunstanville Terrace.

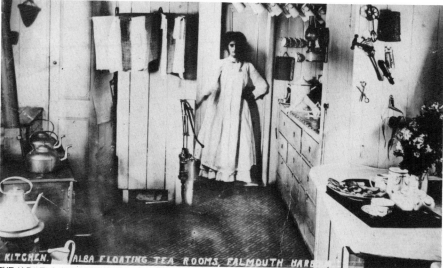

THE ALBA FLOATING TEA ROOMS was a novelty anchored between Pye's Cellars and Flushing for several years before 1914, to which passengers were transported by local watermen from any of the quays along this part of the waterfront. A newspaper advertisement in 1910 proclaimed 'Alba Floating Tea Rooms: Proprietor, A. Whyte. Tea and Cakes 1s. per head. Boats from Prince of Wales' Pier.'

The Harbour

Harbourmouth, Falmouth

THIS PICTURE IS TYPICAL of Falmouth harbour in the days of sail, with four large windjammers anchored on the east side of Black Rock, probably waiting 'for orders' while, leaving the harbour, close in to Little Dennis fortification, are two smaller coastal trading craft. The volume of coastal traffic was very considerable and, before roads and railways took over much of this trade after the First World War, bulk carriage of many types of goods was only possible by sea.

THE FIRST STEAMERS to be seen in Falmouth harbour were probably the steam Packets based on Southampton which, in 1834, began calling here on both outward and homeward journeys to pick up and deliver the mail. In 1837 a steamer, *Ramona*, was based here to intercept homecoming sailing Packets off the Isles of Scilly and bring the mail more quickly to Falmouth. These early steamers also had a sailing capability which they used whenever the wind was favourable. In the second half of the century steam tugs appeared, and their earliest function, as illustrated by the tug here, *Carbon*, was to tow sailing boats such as this topsail schooner out into the open sea where there was usually enough wind to sail away. Later, vessels were built as passenger-tugs, operating as the one in summer and the other in winter; there were, however, several built solely for towage purposes operated by the port's three main shipping agents – Broad, Fox and Deeble – as well as by a number of family businesses such as Rowe, Rusden and Lean. Many of these vessels were built locally by Cox and Co, or by Pool, Skinner and Williams at their yards on the Bar.

ROSELAND WAS BUILT by Cox and Co. for the St Mawes Steam Tug and Passenger Company in 1886 and served on the St Mawes ferry service for about fifty years. In addition to the accommodation seen in the picture, there were two small saloons below deck level, the one at the stern being for ladies and slightly more comfortable than its forward counterpart. *Roseland* is seen here sailing towards Prince of Wales' Pier, with the newly-built mansions along Trefusis Road, Flushing, in the background.

VICTORIA WAS THE SECOND PASSENGER-TUG of that name to be operated by the River Fal Steamship Company, when she was completed by Cox and Co. in 1909 and used between Falmouth and Truro. Return fare was 1s., single 9d., children 6d. But her life in the port was a short one as she was sold to the Portuguese Government in 1905. From the appearance of the ship's wake, she is going astern, away from Prince of Wales' Pier.

THE COASTGUARD LOOKOUT on the top of the keep at Pendennis Castle was closed on 9 January 1909, when the service was reorganized. The time-ball on the mast, erected in 1897, was lowered daily at 1 p.m. so that mariners on vessels in the harbour could adjust their timepieces. Lower down is the storm cone which was raised to warn shipping of approaching gales at lookouts all round the coast up to the early 1980s.

PILOT BOAT 13, said to be the finest operated by the Falmouth Pilot Boat Association, was sunk off the Lizard on 28 April 1905. As was usual in those days, several pilots were carried well south of the Lizard, put on to vessels as required and only three men were left on board when, in fine, clear weather, she was hit and sunk by the large coasting steamer *Milo* of Bristol. The three men were picked up by the *Milo*, put ashore at the Lizard and left to find their own way back to Falmouth.

THE SITING OF A LIGHTHOUSE to indicate the entrance of Falmouth harbour was controversial. Some wanted it on the Manacles and others on Black Rock, but eventually the authorities decided its location should be on St Anthony Head on the east side of the harbour entrance. Building was begun in May 1834 by Olvers of Falmouth, and a notice issued by Trinity House in April 1835 announced that 'a light on St Anthony Point ... will be exhibited on the evening of Monday 20th and thenceforth ... every night from sunset to sunrise.' The light is 65 ft above sea level and was meant to be visible from 13 miles, although vessels at sea reported it could be seen from 16 miles away. After a time it was given a fog signal in the shape of a two-ton bell, the heaviest in Cornwall until it was removed in 1954 and replaced by a fog horn. At considerable trouble the bell was taken to Penwerris Church but, after lying on the lawn there for five years, the expense of installing it was said to be too great and it ended its days in the furnace of a Loughborough bell foundry. As one of the functions of this lighthouse is to warn ships approaching Falmouth of the danger of the Manacles, the sector between 022 and 004 degrees flashes red. This old photograph of the lighthouse shows several large sailing vessels at anchor near the harbour entrance.

HMS *GANGES* ARRIVED IN THE HARBOUR in March 1866 and was anchored in St Just Pool with her administrative establishment ashore in the former Royal Naval Dockyard at Mylor for thirty-three years. Used, like many old naval vessels of her kind, as a training ship for boys, her complement took a full part in the life of the harbour and town: her whalers competed in local regattas, her sports teams competed locally, and her band attended important functions. But life was hard for the boys under training and the names on the large memorial standing at the top of Mylor churchyard testify to the loss of several young lives. At any one time, over 400 boys were under training and it was tough; in fact, it has been suggested that one of the reasons for moving *Ganges* to Falmouth from Devonport was her growing reputation for severe treatment of the boys. Birching over a gun using a switch soaked in brine, was common as daily punishment at 11.40 a.m, when all boys were assembled to witness it. The lower picture shows *Ganges* being towed away by naval tugs on 28 August 1899 to end her days off Shotley where she gave her name to a naval shore training establishment.

FOR TWENTY YEARS, this old two-decker, *Implacable*, which was launched in 1789 and fought at Trafalgar under French colours as the *Duguay Trouin*, lay in Falmouth harbour or King Harry Reach as a holiday ship for boys. In 1855 she had become a naval training ship at Devonport until paid off in 1904. Advertised for sale in 1908, Mr G.E. Wheatley Cobb bought her after long negotiation and several appeals for financial aid, and brought her to Falmouth in 1912. He spent thousands of pounds on her upkeep but, despite help from many quarters, including King George V, the burden proved too great. Together with Revd Christopherson (p. 57) he was awarded the Freedom of the Borough in 1912. Following his death the vessel was taken to Portsmouth in 1932.

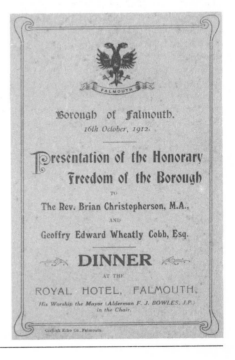

Borough of Falmouth.
16th October, 1912.

Presentation of the Honorary Freedom of the Borough

TO

The Rev. Brian Christopherson, M.A.,

AND

Geoffry Edward Wheatly Cobb, Esq.

DINNER

AT THE

ROYAL HOTEL, FALMOUTH.

*His Worship the Mayor (Alderman F. J. BOWLES, J.P.)
in the Chair.*

THE MOST FAMOUS SAILING SHIP to be anchored in Falmouth harbour was undoubtedly the *Cutty Sark* and, since leaving the port, this beautiful old clipper has attracted tens of thousands of visitors to her dock at Greenwich. Her all-too-brief stay in Falmouth (1923-38) was due to Captain Dowman, himself a master mariner, who saw her storm-bound in the harbour, bought her from her Portuguese owner and restored her as a full rigged clipper ship. On his death his widow presented the ship to the Thames Nautical Training College at Greenhithe. The name *Cutty Sark* means, in English, 'short shirt' and it derived from an ancient Scottish legend told in Robert Burns' poem 'Tam o' Shanter'. When in port the clipper always carried a metallic shirt-shape at her masthead to distinguish her from other clippers. Astern of the Cutty Sark in this picture is *Foudroyant*, the former French frigate *Trincomalee*, owned and renamed by Mr Wheatley Cobb. Used as a training ship for boys until her departure to Portsmouth in 1929, *Foudroyant* is well remembered by older townsfolk, not least for the bugle call which daily resounded over harbour and waterfront at sunset. *Foudroyant* was berthed in Portsmouth after leaving Falmouth. Having recently been completely restored in Hartlepool, she will become an attraction in a maritime museum there as the second oldest warship afloat in the world.

Right:

THE NAME 'WINDJAMMER' was originally a pejorative term used by crews of early steam vessels to describe beautiful square-rigged barques such as the *Herzogin Cecilie*, seen in this photograph in Falmouth Bay. Many such vessels were seen in the harbour from the 1880s up to the Second World War because, as the first large harbour in the Channel, captains would come here to learn from their owners where they should go to unload their cargo and the expression 'Falmouth for Orders' became known all over the world as these ships sailed from South Australia with wheat or coal, South America with guano or nitrate, or the Pacific

north-west of the USA with lumber or grain. Such vessels came into their own when much larger ships could be built of steel as they had the advantages over the early steamships of being cheaper to run, having greater cargo capacity as the hull was not cluttered with engines, and preferring the gale force winds which often put steamships' engines out of action or crumpled their smokestacks; in fact, with a favourable wind, they were faster than the early steamers. Carrying largely non-perishable cargoes, they could remain anchored in Carrick Roads, acting as a floating warehouse until the market for the cargo was more favourable for the owners. In 1883, for example, 3,437 vessels came to Falmouth from overseas, totalling 1,394,934 tons, and newspapers regularly reported arrivals such as '7 heavily laden grain ships arrived in one morning from the Black Sea' (1887), or 'in the past week, 71 vessels have arrived in Falmouth, 30 laden with wheat' (1893). *Herzogin Cecilie* was built in 1902 as a German cadet/cargo ship and ran as such up to 1914 when she rusted for six years in Coquimbo, Chile. Bought in 1921 by the renowned Finnish captain Gustaf Erikson, she made several spectacular runs from Spencer Gulf, Australia with grain to Falmouth, including the journey which inspired Alan Villiers to write his book *Falmouth for Orders*. Then, after an amazing 82-day run from Port Victoria she left Falmouth on 24 April 1936 and seven hours later ran ashore in fog on the coast of South Devon and became a total wreck.

HMS *Torrid* lies aground on Trefusis Point in March 1937 having dragged her anchor. She was under tow to Hayle to be broken up, came into Carrick Roads to shelter from a south-westerly gale and was driven ashore here. She was not refloated but broken up on this site. Not far from this spot one of the worst disasters ever to take place on the Cornish coast happened in January 1814, ironically in one of the world's most sheltered harbours. An army transport, the *Queen*, one of a convoy of eight ships, left Lisbon for Portsmouth carrying 180 soldiers, 63 women, 58 children (soldiers took their families to war in those days), 10 French prisoners and 21 crew ... in total, 332 persons. Rough weather entering the Channel caused the convoy to shelter in Carrick Roads for three days as the weather worsened. During the night the east wind reached hurricane force, accompanied by driving snow, and under these conditions the *Queen's* anchor first dragged, then parted. The wind soon drove her on to the rocks at Trefusis Point where, at about 4.00 a.m, the vessel struck, then broached. Heavy waves crushed the hull, guns broke loose, and rigging entangled everything, with the result that the only survivors were 85 soldiers (some of whom raised the alarm), 9 women, one child, 4 prisoners and 2 crew. Daylight presented a terrible sight of bodies floating in the shallows, cast up on the rocks and entangled in the rigging. A mass grave in Mylor churchyard contains over 130 of the dead with a tombstone bearing the epitaph, 'To the memory of the warriors, women and children who, returning from the coast of Spain unhappily perished in the wreck of the *Queen* transport, on Trefusis Point, January 14th, 1814. This stone is erected as a testimony of regret by the inhabitants of this Parish.' It still acts as a reminder to us of the most disastrous wreck ever to occur in the harbour.

BOTH OF THESE SAILING VESSELS came to grief in the harbour. The Norwegian barque *Velkommen*, above, 360 tons, was on passage in November 1896 from Le Havre to Newport in ballast and under tow. On the way to shelter in Falmouth harbour in an easterly gale the tow parted and the vessel drove ashore alongside Crab Quay at the end of Pendennis Point. The Coastguard rescued the captain's wife and crew of eight by breeches buoy and, after attempts to salvage her failed, she was broken up by W.H. Lean. Below, the four-masted French barque *Asnières* was entering the harbour 'for orders' with a cargo of barley from San Francisco in December 1914, when she went aground on the rocks near St Mawes Castle. At first, there was no danger and the *Bob Newbon* stood by, but two days later a gale blew up and twenty-five crew were taken off by the lifeboat.

TO SAVE LONG JOURNEYS BY LAND, ferries have always been of great importance in branching estuaries such as the Fal. In the early days ferries existed across the mouth of every creek and across important reaches of the main river. At first they consisted of boats' hulls (several lashed together if necessary) which were rowed across after the vehicles and horses (usually separately) had been loaded by planks, as shown at the old Malpas ferry, above. The journey between the Roseland peninsula and the 'mainland' can be made fifteen miles shorter by crossing King Harry Reach and such a 'horse-ferry' existed until 1889 when the King Harry Steam Ferry Co. Ltd installed its first 'ferry-bridge' (shown below) which pulled itself across on chains attached firmly to both banks. Later ferries were larger but the basic principle remained the same and today's ferry, the sixth, was launched in March 1974. Even when diesel engines were installed in 1956 the name of the company was retained, mainly out of sentiment.

BECAUSE OF WARTIME REQUIREMENTS, during the First World War, many ships which would normally have been broken up were kept in operation. Soon after the war, there was an enormous surplus of shipping and much of it was laid up in the various reaches of the Fal. Here (above) several vessels lie abreast just above King Harry Ferry with the second ferry in the foreground and a Criddle and Smith van setting off to somewhere in Roseland. Below, at Tolverne, upstream of the ferry, nine ships lie idle. Other parts of the estuary used for this sad purpose were the Penryn River, Mylor Pool and Tresillian Creek. The River Fal is popular for such laying- up because of the great depth of water well inland, as well as the cost. One victim of a more recent shipping depression was the former liner *Uganda* which became famous as a hospital ship during the Falklands War but was eventually taken to the Far East and broken up.

SAILING SHIPS HAVE USED THE FAL ESTUARY for centuries and these photographs show the two extremes. Above, a fleet of small trading ketches and schooners are raising their sails prior to leaving the harbour, probably having sheltered after a spell of bad weather. Such a departure must have been a magnificent sight as they all sailed out past St Anthony lighthouse and into the bay. Below, three of the huge J-Class yachts, from left to right, *White Heather, Lulworth* and *Britannia*, race off the Cornish coast in 1926. About 80 ft long, the mast over 150 ft high and keel of 60 to 70 tons, these were owned by the very wealthy but they did employ local fishermen in the summer months. Only ten were built and names such as *Enterprise, Shamrock, Endeavour, Velsheda* and *Astra* are still remembered in the port.

Wartime

THE ARRIVAL OF THIS FIRST WORLD WAR TANK (already seen on p. 65) was the subject of municipal celebration. Members of the official welcoming party, including the Borough mace-bearers, are perched precariously on top while the spectators, including a youth band, stand admiringly on the Moor. The Market House and Trevethan Board School are in the background.

SINCE ITS COMPLETION IN 1543, the keep of Pendennis Castle was the focus of military activity in the town until soon after the Second World War, but if this photograph appears different from the castle we know today, it is because the single-storey gatehouse on the left has been demolished. Built originally to defend the harbour entrance, the castle has fulfilled that role in a variety of ways, the method of coastal defence changing through the centuries. Since the end of the Napoleonic Wars except during periods of war, the castle has been used by the 'part-time' army, first the Militia and then, after 1908, the Territorial Army. Of the former, the unit which used the defences most regularly was the Cornwall and Devon Miners Royal Garrison Artillery Militia, understandably abbreviated to the Royal Miners. The officers were local gentry, the NCOs mostly regular soldiers and the men came from anywhere. They included many Irishmen who came to the castle for a period up to nine weeks to be trained, for which they were, of course, paid. During periods of militia training there was regularly trouble in the town after closing-time at weekends, when trainees had been paid. Eventually this disorder reached such an alarming scale that militiamen were paid at the railway station immediately prior to their departure.

THIS PHOTOGRAPH, taken at the Half Moon Battery in 1867, shows the officers of the Royal Miners assembled for training. They were, back row, from left to right: Capt. Borlase, Lt. Rasleigh, Lt. Horsford. Front row, standing: Lt. Mitchell, Lt. Polwhele, Dr Bullmore, Major Champion, Capt. Sawle, RSM Griffin, Capt. Howell. Front row, sitting: Col. Rashleigh, Lt. Pomeroy, Capt. Clarke. Both the newly-gazetted lieutenants in the back row eventually assumed command of the regiment.

THIS PHOTOGRAPH of the whole regiment of Royal Miners on parade in 1873 inside the castle enclosure gives an idea of the number of men involved in such training. The bell-tents in the background were officers' accommodation; other ranks camped on the Hornworks. Although in the early years the Officers' Mess was in one of the town's hotels (Falmouth, Royal or Greenbank), a mess building was later erected on the Hornworks.

ON THE OUTBREAK of the First World War German vessels at sea had no idea that hostilities had commenced and sailed on, many of them coming to Falmouth 'for orders' and capture by the Royal Navy. As the *Western Morning News* of 11 September, 1914 reported, 'The German four-master barque *Goldbek*, 2,467 tons, Tacoma for London with wheat, arrived at Falmouth yesterday. She was captured by a British cruiser and a prize crew placed aboard. Off the Lizard the tug *Triton* took her in tow. She carried a crew of twenty-two. A British cruiser yesterday also captured the German ship *Orlando*, 2,065 tons, from Mexillones for Falmouth for orders. She has 2,300 tons of nitrate on board worth £15 per ton.'

PONUS, A 5,077-TON EARLY OIL TANKER went ashore on the rocks between Swanpool and Gyllyngvase beaches on 13 November 1916, having dragged her anchor in a gale. Most of the crew got off in the ship's boats and soon afterwards the vessel caught fire and burned for three days, pouring oil on to water which also ignited as shown in the photograph. Several successive salvage efforts have removed most of the wreck but some may still be seen in the shallows at low spring tide.

THIS CROWDED SCENE on Gyllyngvase beach in September 1915, was a fund-raising event. During the First World War, after any one of the several terrible battles in the trenches of northern France and Flanders, some casualties were brought to Falmouth and local schools and halls were used as temporary hospitals. This gala occasion was organized to raise money for the War Field Hospitals Supply Unit and entailed swimming events, including a long-distance race from St Anthony Head to Gyllyngvase, band concerts (one is in progress, left of centre, in the photograph) and, as the banner proclaims, afternoon teas were served. Many local people helped the troops in many ways at these times: sports events, including bowls, were organized, canteens were opened in many local venues including the churches and the Polytechnic Hall, and many soldiers were given hospitality in homes all over the town.

THE GERMAN SUBMARINE OFFENSIVE was launched in an attempt to blockade Britain and cut off our essential imports after 1915. One of several counter-measures was the establishment at Bonython, on the flat top of the Lizard peninsula, of an RAF base for airships such as these. As they were comparatively quiet, their aim was to catch the U-boats on the surface and drop hand-held bombs on them, patrolling the seas around west Cornwall and the 'western approaches'. It is not surprising that in the high winds experienced in that exposed position, mishaps occurred such as that shown below. The massive hangar erected to house the airship is also shown.

THE STEEL, THREE-MASTED SCHOONER *Mary B. Mitchell* was built in Northern Ireland in 1892 for Baron Penrhyn of Beaumaris. In April 1916 she was commandeered in Swansea and brought to Falmouth for fitting out as a decoy or Q-ship, renamed HMS *Mitchell* (Q9), but referred to locally as 'MBM'. The idea was simple but required nerves of steel to achieve its aim. Under various disguises the vessel sailed around the coast and into the Channel and Atlantic, giving the appearance of an innocent trading schooner, until a U-boat, not willing to waste a torpedo on so small a target, surfaced to destroy it by gunfire. When the submarine was within range, the deckhouses would be swiftly collapsed to reveal one twelve-pounder (seen in the picture above) and two six-pounder guns and fire would be opened on the enemy. Far-fetched though all this may seem, it really worked and the routine often involved a 'panic crew' taking to the lifeboat and rowing away to give the impression of abandoning ship when the U-boat appeared. The Germans were trying to prevent coastal shipping from operating and many genuine coastal schooners were sunk by gunfire or by explosive charges placed aboard after interception, although on one patrol MBM sank two submarines in one day. The first followed the Q-ship from a range of three miles at first, later closing to one mile and opening fire. Not one German shell hit MBM, which only opened fire when the U-boat was well within range, hitting the conning tower with her first round after which seven more direct hits sank the enemy vessel. Later, another U-boat opened fire from two miles and the 'panic crew' took to the lifeboat, making her appear abandoned; approaching carefully both on the surface and submerged, the submarine finally began to surface a mere fifty yards away and MBM's first shot hit her. With an explosion, the U-boat sank immediately. Altogether the Q-ship sank at least four U-boats and during her career as a decoy ship, she sailed under British, French and Russian colours, changing her appearance after each action. Several times she was challenged by patrol boats from Falmouth which did not recognize her and this method of warfare proved so successful that other sailing craft were sent to Falmouth for conversion to Q-ships. Not surprisingly, several of MBM's crew of three officers and thirty ratings were awarded gallantry medals and on 6 December 1918, HMS *Mitchell* was tied up alongside Prince of Wales' Pier and opened to the public for eight days, during which time she sold £36,000 worth of War Bonds. After this she was allowed to resume her civilian life.

PROBABLY BECAUSE THE GERMAN VESSELS WERE SUPERIOR to those in the Royal Navy at that time, eight German submarines, captured after the First World War, were brought to Falmouth in 1921 with a specially constructed lifting vessel *Cyklops*, seen below, so that experts could examine them and discover their secrets. Four were tested to destruction in the bay and, when the tests were completed, eye-witnesses testify to the deliberate abandoning of the others on the rocks on the west side of Pendennis Point: they were, probably, UBs 54, 86, 96 and 112. They lay there as a tourist attraction and playground for local youngsters until the early days of the Second World War when they were broken up by Harris Brothers for scrap.

THE GERMAN TRAINING BATTLESHIP *SCHLESWIG HOLSTEIN* visited Falmouth as part of a 'goodwill' cruise around Britain in 1938 and 1939. Members of the crew were entertained by the townsfolk, an 'act of Christian Fellowship' was shared at Falmouth parish church with the singing of English and German hymns, and the crew were allowed to roam all over the town, armed with cameras the like of which few of us had ever seen. By September 1939 the same vessel was firing the first shots of the Second World War at point blank range into the city of Danzig.

FALMOUTH WAS BOMBED FREQUENTLY after June 1940 and for a short time it was the most-bombed town in Britain; in fact, a member of the Borough Council was reported in the press to have said that Cornwall was proud to be fighting alongside England in the war! Many attempts were made to hit the docks but few succeeded until 10 July 1940 when, as the photograph shows, in a daylight raid, three ships alongside the northern arm were hit. *Maria Chandris*, a Greek steamer, was loaded with raw cotton which burned furiously. Local tugs managed to get a line aboard and tow the vessel over to St Mawes where she was beached on Amsterdam Point at the mouth of Place Creek. *British Chancellor* did not appear too badly damaged until the fire reached her magazine which blew up with an enormous explosion. *Tuscalusa*, having taken two direct hits, was blazing from midships to stern and towed to St Just Pool where she too was beached. *Maria Chandris* and *Tuscalusa* were both cut up for scrap later in the war. There were casualties among ships' crews and dockyard workers, and survivors who had escaped to the northern breakwater found their route cut off because the wooden jetty was on fire. They had to be rescued by tugs and lifeboats.

Above right:
THE TOWN WAS BOMBED on several occasions and the Methodist Church on the Moor was hit twice. During one of these raids, on 12 May 1941, Trevethan Board School was also severely damaged and reduced to the state shown here. Most of it was later demolished as unsafe, but the clock tower stood alone on the hillside for several years until it, too, was demolished.

Below right:
MANY OF THE SEA-FRONT HOTELS were taken over for use by the armed forces during the war and in one raid on 30 May 1944, the Pentargan and Boscawen were badly damaged and several people were killed. Altogether, enemy action in Falmouth killed 31 and injured 91 people; 39 houses were demolished and 1,932 damaged.

IN THE PRE-WAR ATMOSPHERE of 1939, many young men joined the Territorial Army and here, a group of former Grammar School pupils is about to depart from Falmouth station for training. They are, left to right: 'Stinker' Pugh, Frank Bennetts, 'Berbie' Hughes, 'Morrie' Osborne, 'Grub' Rundle, 'Splits' Belletti, 'Porker' Johns and Freddie Truscott.

FUND-RAISING EVENTS took place regularly during the war to persuade people to invest in war-savings and in this photograph, a 'Wings for Victory Week' campaign is about to start outside the Town Hall on the Moor with a parade of all branches of the armed forces and local service and voluntary organizations.

A GROUP OF LARGELY UNSUNG HEROES who did much of the dirty work of clearing up the mess after air raids is photographed here. The Falmouth Rescue and Decontamination Squad was composed mostly of workers employed by the Borough Council but not all are present here as there was confusion over the date and only these men turned up to be photographed. They are, back row, left to right: R. Harris, E. May, C. Merryfield, F. Pedley, H. Dash, L. Webber, C. Watts, R. Bolitho. Middle row: M. Johns, C. Berryman, J. Gilbert, W. Barnicoat, H. Vinson, J. Pascoe, G. Thomas, H. Snell. Front row: T. Trevillion, J. Edgcumbe, C. Dawe (foreman), H.E. Tresidder (in charge), R.H. Lewarne BEM (second in charge), W. Maynard, J. Smale.

BARRAGE BALLOONS began to make their appearance in the skies over Falmouth in 1940, both on land and attached to tenders, often former coastal trading schooners, in the harbour. In this photograph the balloon site on the Beacon is backed by the large American Quonset hut, used as a mess hall.

AFTER THE DUNKIRK EVACUATION in 1940, preparations for a German invasion included the formation of the Local Defence Volunteers (LDV), later renamed the Home Guard. In these two photographs, members of the 7th Battalion are seen in two contrasting roles and a careful inspection will reveal the same faces in both pictures. The Battalion Officers above are, back row, left to right: CSM Marsden, Max Richards, B. Thomas, Fred Chambers, Jack Curtis, J. Parkes, -?- , Jim Treen, CSM Jack Salisbury. Middle row: ? Carlyle, Ivan Lake, Arthur Hillman, Percy Bowers, Arthur Downing, Wesley Hosken, Jack Wenman, D. Richards. Front row: Clem Richards, Reg Pearce, Archie Robins, Bill Collins, Major Stafford Hough, A.T. Carter, Bob Brobson, T. Miller, Reg Veal. Below, in a break during a training exercise the guardsmen relax with refreshment from the Redruth Brewery.

ROBERT HICHENS – or 'Hich' as he was known to his fellow sailors – was a Cornishman raised in Flushing who spent much of his boyhood sailing the waters of Falmouth harbour. He became a solicitor and joined the firm of Reginald Rogers & Son in Falmouth. His interest in sailing continued as a member of the Royal Cornwall Yacht Club and he added driving fast cars in the Le Mans 24-hour race to his sporting achievements. He commenced active service with the RNVR in October 1939, and by 1942 had become a member of an efficient fighting force of Motor Gun Boats acting around the coast of Britain, mainly in the North Sea but also in the English Channel. Their wide-ranging activities included attacking German E-Boats whenever they could be brought to battle, protecting convoys of merchant vessels around our coast, attacking enemy convoys and lying in ambush outside Continental harbours for E-Boats returning from operations. Lt.-Com. Hichens was instrumental in developing the tactics responsible for the outstanding success of these small boat operations and showed his great qualities of leadership and courage to such an extent that the men in his command were not afraid of going into action, but of not reaching the high standard expected of them by 'Hich'. After many successful operations, for which he was awarded two DSOs, three DSCs, and was mentioned in despatches three times, he wrote a book, published in 1944, entitled *We Fought Them in Gunboats*, necessarily heavily censored but giving an excellent description of the problems, tension, excitement, disappointment and discomfort involved in small boat fighting. He made it abundantly clear in the book that, throughout his naval career, he had great contempt for two categories of people: senior officers and shore staff who showed a total lack of appreciation of the problems and requirements of the fighting sailors; and some inefficient but ambitious politicians whose direction of the war seemed totally lacking in any understanding of the realities of the combat situation. Neither did he look kindly upon those civilian dockyard workers who were prepared to go on strike during wartime for trifling reasons, especially as they were earning ten times more than some of his sailors whose lives were constantly at risk. The book was never finished. He fought many actions that he did not live to write about. On 13 April 1943, after a minor engagement with the enemy had been broken off, Lt.-Com. Hichens was killed by a stray shell.

AS PART OF THE PREPARATION FOR THE D-DAY INVASION OF FRANCE, in 1943 the United States Navy arrived in Falmouth to establish an Advanced Amphibious Base in the fields to the west of the Beacon. The main entrance to the base (above) was at the end of Tregothnan Road; the Camp itself ran down beside Dracaena Avenue (below) and spread across the top of the Beacon. Several local girls became the naval equivalent of 'GI Brides' and the US personnel quickly integrated into Falmouth society. Several of the men still correspond regularly with friends in the town and visit Falmouth to relive their wartime memories and revisit old haunts. Much of our photographic collection of this aspect of Falmouth's past has come from this source.

MUCH OF THE ESTUARY OF THE FAL was used by the US Navy in its build-up for the D-Day invasion in June 1944, and many different types of craft appeared in the harbour. Above, tank landing craft lie alongside the Empire Wharf in the docks where much of the essential repair and maintenance was carried out. The reclaimed land in front of Grove Place was taken over by the naval maintenance teams as workshops and in the official US photograph, below, a tank landing craft embarks an Armoured Recovery Vehicle, an obsolete General Lee tank fitted with a crane and powerful winches to recover disabled tanks on the battlefield. The high structure to the rear of the vehicle is deep wading trunking enabling it to come ashore in six feet of water.

WHEN THE WAR IN EUROPE WAS OVER celebrations were in order. The photograph above shows a street party in progress in Berkeley Cottages and many local people will recognize themselves or their friends and relatives in it. The shelter below, on Falmouth sea front, was presented to the town by US Naval personnel and on the floor is set a plaque which states, 'Presented by the Officers and Men of the US Naval Advanced Amphibious Base, Falmouth, Cornwall, 1943–1944. Cmdr. Lawrence W. Snell USNR Commanding Officer'.

Other Places

THESE CHILDREN STAND at what was once the end of New Street which, after the main street, is one of the town's oldest. Behind them, beside the parish church, is the old graveyard and, beyond it, Porhan Street, another very old part of the town. In the 1960s the two streets were joined by continuing the road through the graveyard and the authorities encountered many problems with the old graves, some of which dated back to the seventeenth century.

A REPORT TO THE GENERAL BOARD OF HEALTH in 1854 into the sanitary state of the Borough observed 'the state of the churchyard ... is such as to render the decent interment ... altogether impossible and ... must be injurious, if not absolutely dangerous, to the health of those residing nearby', and went on, 'the depth of graves varies ... often being less than five feet; coffins are ... invariably exposed whenever a grave is made. The soil of the churchyard is very full of human remains ... after a heavy shower bones may be seen on the surface. With a view to partially remedy this and to prevent the effluvia which is said to arise from the churchyard some hundreds of loads of earth have from time to time been wheeled into and spread over the churchyard.' It is not surprising, therefore, that under the guidance of Revd W.J. Coope a new graveyard was established well out of the town on the hilltop overlooking Swanpool in 1857.

EVEN WHEN PIPED WATER HAD BEEN SUPPLIED – at a price – to parts of Falmouth from reservoirs in the College Valley of Penryn after the founding of the Waterworks Company by James Blatch Cox in 1847, much of the town's water supply continued to come from wells or pumps such as this, the Beehive Pump, dated 1840, in Porhan Street. This, combined with the total lack of any system of sewage disposal, led to serious outbreaks of cholera as recently as 1852 and dysentry in 1902. At about the latter date Falmouth was being widely advertised as a health resort.

PORHAN STREET contained some impressive houses, built mostly in the eighteenth century, but as their occupants moved to the more salubrious parts of the town, the houses became slums with somewhat primitive drainage and water supply. Most were demolished in a slum clearance scheme of the early 1930s.

MILL ROW, seen from Swanpool Street, got its name from the mill which once stood on the site of the Friends' Meeting House, the end of which is seen at the far end of the Row. This mill was part of the ill-fated scheme, devised by Peter Killigrew (II) but thwarted by the Corporation, to bring a water supply to the quays below, using water brought along a leat from the Swanpool valley. A mill-pool was established on the hillside above and this would have supplied water to drive the mill which stood here up to the early nineteenth century. This site is now occupied by a lawn and gardens between New Street and Gyllyng Street.

AT ONE TIME Lake's Directory listed three places called Gutheridge's Yard. This one was one of the four 'courts' to lead off from the north side of Well Lane – the others were Berth's Court, Rose Cottages and Sedgmond's Court. The cobbled pathway, granite-lined drains and natural stone walls combine to give such rows of late-eighteenth-century housing a quaint appearance, but they were in fact rather dark, insanitary hovels in which disease was rife on account of their totally inadequate sewage disposal and water supply facilities. They were demolished in the slum clearances of the 1930s.

THE TOWN QUARRY AND QUARRY HILL leading to it were once the location of a number of small, family industries housed in wooden sheds, which were tarred for preservative reasons, such as this workshop of H.S. Hancock, builder and undertaker. Others included two blacksmiths (E. Dunstan and J. Tiddy), Grigg's, monumental mason, two sets of stables (J.H. Coleman and E.B. Williams), G. Flint's marine stores and Alfred Webb, domestic engineer and china and glass rivetter. The Town Quarry is one of eleven such excavations to have existed within the old Borough boundary; some have been obliterated by subsequent development. Apart from the obvious ones – Town, Windsor and Penwerris Lane – smaller ones or their remains may still be seen at Pike's Hill, Gyllyngdune Gardens, inside the docks, Trelawney Road, Ashfield and Pennance, all having been used to supply building material or rubble for road making.

FALMOUTH'S EARLIEST RECORDED HOSPITAL overlooked Swanpool Beach, somewhere near the end of what is now Boscawen Road, and was probably for those from ships in the harbour with infectious diseases. Later, a small private hospital occupied 1 Albert Cottages but the first Falmouth Hospital, which incorporated the dispensary moved from Church Street, was built in 1893 at the top of Killigrew Road (above). The foundation stone had been laid by benefactor, Mr J. Passmore Edwards who, soon afterwards, was accorded the Freedom of the Borough on account of his generosity. As the town grew, other benefactors were responsible for both the land and the building of a larger hospital (below) on the outskirts of the town overlooking the Swanpool valley. Two Cornish residents of Johannesburg, William Mountstephens and Albert Charles Collins, donated the money and the new hospital was opened in April 1930. It has recently suffered in the way of all cottage hospitals with the centralization of medical services.

ASHFIELD, between Ponsharden and Turnpike Creeks, on the road from Penryn was, like Penwerris, part of Budock parish up to 1892. The Stephens family lived in Ashfield House and set up the ropeworks of John Stephens and Son Ltd, seen above, including the long ropewalk stretching off to the left of the photograph. Their products included wire rope for mining and shipping, 'Lighthouse' brand manilla rope for shipping and 'Sickle' brand hemp rope and twine for general purposes, especially binder twine for agriculture. The works, residence, grounds and farm covered thirty acres and at its peak employed 150 men. The cottages seen to the right were built for employees in the works and beyond them was a public house, the Bassett Arms. The ropeworks closed down in the early 1930s when taken over by British Ropes who continued to use the buildings as a distribution centre for their products for some years.

AS THE TOWN EXPANDED INLAND from the harbour, access to the new, largely residential areas became difficult, especially with the impact of the internal combustion engine. In 1922/3 a new approach road was built from Ashfield to the Recreation Ground, through the fields of Ashfield and Penwerris farms on the nearside of the ropeworks seen on the opposite page. The steep slope at the top of the hill required a cutting to be dug through the fields occupied by the town's golf course and the picture above shows how such an operation was executed in those days – with shovels, horses and carts! Ashfield 'settlement' can be seen in the background. The new road (below) was opened on 14 February 1923 by the mayor, Mr John Harris, and the crowd walked back along the road into Falmouth. The houses behind the official party are those built for workers in the nearby ropeworks.

ACKNOWLEDGEMENTS

There is no better place in which to live, work and bring up a family than Falmouth and this book is a very small gesture of my gratitude to the town and its people for my having been able to do those things. Many helpful friends have contributed in various ways to its completion, if only by nagging me constantly to write it, but those I should especially like to thank for more practical kinds of assistance are:

Joan Berntzen • Pam Harvey • Kathleen Hoare • Sylvia Peters
Lady Ursula Redwood • John Beck • Ernie Binham • Harry Binham
Bob Cox • Phil Dyer • Gerald Eddy • Tony Eddy • Ted Fisher
Keith Hancock • Dick Jeffery • George Laity • John Marquis• Phil Mitchell
David Mudd MP • Maurice Osborne • Bob Paterson • Jim Pearce
André le Person • Tom Stroud • Alan Symonds • Bert Thomas
David Trevarthen • Tony Warren and Ken Williams

Two dear friends who did not live to see this work published but have helped and encouraged throughout were Doris Berryman and Fisher Barham. My wife has been a tower of strength in reading, criticizing and commenting on the contents as well as putting up with the untidiness around the house which work of this kind causes me to create! And in all my contacts with the staff of Alan Sutton, particularly Simon Thraves and Louise Kirby, nothing but the friendliest of help and advice has been forthcoming.

There are bound to be statements that some of my fellow Falmothians do not entirely agree with but I feel I can justify all I have written. Selecting 219 out of over 2,000 photographs has not been easy and many I should have liked to include have been omitted. I have only used pictures which have appeared in similar publications when I have something new to say about them; otherwise, I have tried to make the selection as original as possible, provided it is relevant to the Falmouth story. I hope that this volume may persuade some of my townsfolk to delve in drawers and boxes, to search in attics and trunks and to blow the dust from long-forgotten albums and to share their pictures and knowledge. Only then can we make further discoveries about the wonderful town in which we live.